During the period 1820 /25, the owner of the Royal Oak Ale House had painted on his wall a picture showing his boat. It is a unique painting as it shows both Martello Towers and it is the only known picture of the Battery where the Pier Hotel is now. Whilst it has the Trinity Tower, and the Walton Windmill, the Church is believed to be the one that he knew, as no other Church anywhere within the Area looked like this, and it is considered to be the only picture of Kirby Church that is known prior to rebuilding in 1833. Line drawing from original. Possibly painted by Robert Sayer

SETTING
THE
RECORD
STRAIGHT

A CONCISE HISTORY
OF
FRINTON , GREAT HOLLAND,
KIRBY AND WALTON

by

KEN PALMER

TAKE FIVE PUBLISHING

PHOTOGRAPHS ON COVER:

FRONT COVER: WALTON PIER . PROBABLY THE BEST KNOWN
    PICTURE OF THE PIER. c1905
BACK COVER: TOP: KIRBY LE SOKEN, SHOWING OXBORROWS THE
    BLACKSMITHS c1908
MIDDLE: FRINTON. THE MOST WELL KNOWN PHOTOGRAPH OF ST.
    MARY'S. THE BUILDING ON THE RIGHT IS MISSING IN MOST PRINTS,
    WHICH IS FRINTON HALL c1873
BOTTOM: GREAT HOLLAND SHOWING THE RED LION INN. NOW KNOWN
    AS THE LIONS DEN c1908

Copyright: TAKE FIVE PUBLISHING 1994

First published 1994 by Take Five Publishing
15, Raglan Rd, Frinton Essex CO139HH

Printed by

Ipswich Book Company Ltd
The Drift. Nacton Road. Ipswich
Suffolk   1P3 9QR

British Library Cataloguing in Publication Data

Palmer Ken
Frinton, Great Holland, Kirby and Walton
A Concise History. Setting the Record Straight
1 History.
I. Palmer Ken
942.672

ISBN 0 - 9524275 - 0 - 8

LAND CHANGES OVER FOUR HUNDRED YEARS

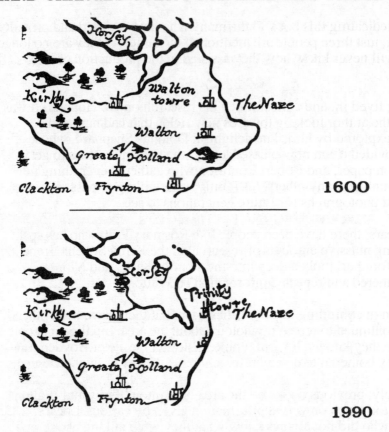

The top map is amongst the earliest which showed this area in any detail and is a direct copy. The bottom map has been altered to comply with that original early map, as the cartographers (map makers) of yesteryear, were not as precise as those of today, and it has been altered slightly in it's shape to show exactly how the Sea has eroded the coast over the past 400 years. HORSEY before 1600 was a large land mass with rivers cutting across it. Now, as is shown, in the 1990's, it is an Island getting smaller each year.

FORWARD and DEDICATION

Instead of dedicating this book to the many who have assisted and provided information, just three people are mentioned by name. As they are no longer alive they will never know how they assisted in the production of this edition.

K D Crook, lived in, and concentrated his research on Gt. Holland. It was he who set the author looking towards new fields that had not been previously explored by him. The delightful Douglas Shephard, whose nagging provided (I am now pleased to say) the first inCentives to get something on paper, and Robert Robinson who gathered everything he could, and, unlike many others, his family were willing to pass all his research and photographs for future generations to see.

In recent years, there have been people like Rosmary Pratt who has spent months doing massive amounts of research on the Kirby Sokens. Irene Johnson before her, looked deep into the story of Kirby and Nipper Norman gathered and repeated information on Walton.

The problem in compiling this book, has been that there have been others who have continued to repeat mythology about the area. Intelligent people who believe they know a lot, but, unlike historian Dr. Peter Boyden, few have actually bothered to do any research to justify any of their statements.

Unfortunately, previous books on the area of Frinton, Kirby and Walton have relied too much on verbal information given by various 'Local Historians' who did not always know what they were talking about, and why this book contains and compiles many hundreds of hours spent questioning everything that has been stated in the past. In it's way, this is a stepping stone for others to see and use, and within these pages there has been included for the first time, new detail and some new theories. Alternate possibilities and arguments. The new information has been double and even triple checked as to it's authenticity. This book seeks to set the Record Straight as there are still too many unanswerables that need solving.

For many years, statements have continually been repeated which are now shown to be often based unsubstantiated and ill researched information. Too many past authors have found it easy, simply to copy the words of others, and by so doing, assist in perpetuating the fiction.

This book attempts to alleviate and correct many, if not all of the errors on FRINTON, GT. HOLLAND, KIRBY and WALTON and readers will find that, in addition, it will offer a past they will have been unaware of. It was originally suggested that anything dealing with this part of the country would be easy to put together, and yet there are has been for centuries an overall lack of written material available. As was found, there are not that many documents covering the period up to the early 17th Century.

Britain was invaded in 1066. This was the last time anyone attacked us and won on home ground, and the Normans led by William arrived. He decided to do a roll call by creating the Domesday Book. A large stockbook of the country. Over the next five hundred years, hundreds of thousands of manuscripts were written and some larger towns have quantities going back centuries. Places like Walton, Kirby, Gt. Holland and Frinton, have few. Changes of land ownership. The occasional Rector taking over a Church. A thief being caught and hung. These are all that remain. Unfortunately, over the years, too many items have been lost or destroyed when fire or war have created the destruction of so much.

The clerks of yesterday only kept documents which they thought may be needed in the future. They were not to know, nor would they have been interested to know, that in a thousand years, people would be questioning how the ordinary man lived, and that Bills and Invoices would take on as much interest as do the Ecclesiastical and legal papers that remain. It is easy to point at those dark ages, centuries ago, and express an attitude of dispair as to why such a small amount seems to have been retained, but gathering information from any period can be difficult, and surprisingly, it has to be shown that establishing fact from fiction within modern history can be as difficult. Newspaper Libraries are normally a fine source of research but even they have their limitations based on what was considered to be news.

6

An example. Between Frinton and Walton two modern buildings and a fine swimming pool opened in the early 1930's. This was called THE LIDO. Yet it's existance was not mentioned in any local paper. It's exact date of opening is therefore unknown. It's closure date is unknown. A leaflet exists showing it's sale in 1935, yet no mention was given as to the outcome of this sale. If it were not for photographs of the place, the Lido might have been passed over as a figment of peoples imaginations, yet in the Round Gardens at Walton, for less than a year during this same period, a 'Road House' opened, yet it's name, and even it's memory are now long gone. Like the Lido, this place is mentioned in the Diaries of a few that actually visited it, but it was not considered worthy enough to be included in a write up in any newspaper.

Over many years writers have repeated what others have stated earlier. Right or wrong makes no matter, and so errors and fantasies continue to be indicated and often quoted as fact. An example of the most common is seen in dozens of books and articles which state that 'old Walton Church fell into the sea in 1798'. Yet had any of these authors bothered to check, they would have found it was only the roof that collapsed in 1798. It is possible a section of walling was to fall down in the late December but this is unconfirmed, for it took a further six years before it was to go completly, and then only because some of it was knocked down and used as foundations for the new Church, which was opened in 1804.

The Urban District Council have repeated a similar myth for nearly thirty years when they have stated in their holiday brochures that Kirby Church has a 13th Century Tower, whilst that seen is a Victorian facing, and no major work on Church Architecture suggests anything else. One book indicates that the upper level is from the 17th Century whilst the lower section is 15th

The Church shown opposite the frontis page, was copied from a painting still existing in Kirby, and produced during the period 1825/1830. The montage combines the two Walton Martello Towers. Trinity Tower and in the same picture, a unique illustration of the Battery in front of the Martello Tower which stood where the Round Gardens now the stands, yet it is the Church that is important, as this was painted within a very short distance of Kirby Church. There was no Church anywhere in the area like this to be seen. Accordingly this is probably the only existing picture of the church at Kirby, prior to it's re-building in 1833.

Therefore to gather the information for this book has been a problem. Many people have helped. A lot of books, both ancient and modern have been read. Much that has been written in the past by others, has been re-examined. Yet, at the end of the day a degree of guesswork and logic has still had to be used to attain some of the answers.

Understanding the background of why things happened has been paramount. To correct specific points has been the aim. Once Connaught Avenue was classified as the 'Bond Street of East Anglia', but this situation may have lasted into the late 1950's, but Frinton, like the world has changed, and the days that had created the 'Bond Street of East Anglia', have long gone.

How many are aware of who it was that really made Frinton the exclusive 'in' place pre-war. It wasn't Peter Bruff who bought land, in order to develop it, nor Richard Powell Cooper who actually created the Town, but Edward, the Prince of Wales, who came to visit and returned many times. He was followed by the 'bright young things' of Society. Already there were millionaires living quietly in Frinton, and more followed. The upper strata of the Theatre and Cinema came to stay, as did diplomates and Members of the Government.

It was the Twenties. Enjoyment and escapism. Tennis and Golf stars flocked to Frinton to play and be seen by Royalty, as both Prince Edward and his brother Prince George started visiting. So did the friends and the hangers on to the Royal couple, and Frinton became the 'in' place, where anyone, who thought they were anyone, had to be.

8

Once King George V died, things changed. Edward abdicated and married the divorcee Mrs Wallace Simpson. Neither his brother nor he returned to Frinton again, ensuring the lichpins that had made Frinton what it was, had gone, and the 'in' crowd headed for Le Touquet or the South of France prior to the start of the last war.

During those 'Royal' years the local newspapers did not mention either Prince Edward or Prince George, as there was an unwritten code of ethics within the Press, and Royalty were left alone unless they were on Official business, and it seems that because of this, Frinton wasn't mentioned too often, other than events like the Tennis week or the Horticultural shows. The day to day running of the Town was passed over because it may have brought in sightseers, and this nobody wanted. The 'exclusive' tag, still regularly used about Frinton, was at that time created.

Events where Gracie Fields sang or Gladys Cooper worked for Charity were never mentioned. An example of the press attitude towards the Royals was that every journalist knew about Edward and Mrs Simpson from the very beginning of their affair, and yet, whilst the story appeared overseas, not one word was ever printed in the British Newspapers until the announcement of their proposed marriage was given. Their privacy was accepted. A pity such attitudes do not exist today.

As far as it is known, neither Walton, Kirby nor Great Holland had any star names, but at the end of the Season, it was the people that remained after the visitors had left, that really mattered. It has been the Polleys, Oxborrows, Salmons and Brooks. The Halls, Sparlings and the Oxleys who made the place vibrant. The Lifeboat crews who risked their lives in all weathers. All of these people, and those with local family histories that go back a hundred or even two hundred years, are what WALTON, KIRBY, GREAT HOLLAND AND FRINTON are all about, and without them there would have been no past, and in turn, no book.

Chapter 1   WHATS IN A NAME

It would be very easy to start this and repeat everything that 'experts' have quoted in the past. Yet, many of these creative talents have seen only what they wanted to see, and everything that has been repeated from then on has been taken to be correct. Unfortunately, because of the complexity, it is not a simple matter of trying to evaluate the names of places where nothing written exists.

What creates these problems is the Saxons in their wisdom changed many of the place names that had been exisiting under the Romans. There are numerous Town names we use today throughout the country that have a Saxon link, yet, on the Coastline there were changes or alterations when the Danes came in their long boats and created havoc, and they too provided new names, a number of which the Saxons continued to use. The Normans from 1066 did their best in retaining many of these place names that originated prior to their arrival, but in the Domesday Book there are a number of spelling differences, and some further changes were to happen because of this.

During the years before the Normans took over, there were many problems and segments of the earlier race of British (known as the Welsh) had been pushed into various pockets of the countryside by the Romans. They were eventually to settle and live alongside the Saxons who had overrun the Country. To try and understand in the simplest terms these problems, the 'Victoria History of the County of Essex' Vol. 2 Pages 259/260 gives enough to show things are really difficult to place into perspective.

There were Royal connections, even around a thousand years ago. Holland in Essex, centuries before it was split into Great and Little Holland, was to be linked with King Arthurs name, as well as King Edward the Elder and King Edgar and then around the year 930/940 AD the Estate comprising of Walton, Thorpe and Kirby is believed to have been given to St. Pauls Church (Cathedral) in London by King Athelston. Part of Frinton was owned by King Harold in the 1020's.

Although this has been written about, much of it is still guesswork because few original documents from these early days, other than the one produced by William and known as the Domesday Book and completed in 1086 which still exists.

The existing St. Pauls library does contain a reasonable amount of documents, but there are few regarding the Walton, Kirby and Thorpe lands owned by them and these show clearly that the Monks and Clerks wrote as they heard. They didn't ask for spellings, but simply wrote as they thought a name sounded. There were in those days, no maps, nor 'place name' lists that they could make reference too.

WALTON, linked with KIRBY and THORPE, and as a single Estate which included the Naze, had been given the name Eadulvesnaesa. Whether this overall parcel of land was owned by someone with this name, is quite unknown, but the spelling was altered by the scribes who wrote the names as they heard, to read Eadolfesnaesse (1049) and in the Domesday book a completly different spelling again was produced by the Normans, Aedulvesnasa. Changes by 1154 to Edulvesnasa and again eighty years later it had been Eduluenase in 1235 and in 1255 Edolvenesse. It has been suggested that this area of land, from Walton to Thorpe could have been owned by a warlord or warrior named Eadwulf or Eadulf or Edulues, and this also included the 'Naesa' (the Naze). There are though a number of Historians who stress the name was definitely Aedulvanasa, yet this is made without any foundation.

'Waltonia' is mentioned as a place name in 1181 and for the next two hundred years it was to change to Waltona, Waltune and Waltaune, and it was only during the late 1300's, that the name we use today was occasionally used, yet it is certainly difficult to ascertain how the name Walton was obtained. Ton or Tun translates to being a Town or Village. An enclosure, a fence, a dwelling or a Farm. A number of choices. There are a total of 28 Walton's in Britain, and many gained their name from being 'Walled Towns'. None of the existing records mentioning our Walton, indicates a Wall or a high surround of earth, but this is not to say it did not exist. It is very possible that a high mound of earth was placed in position to either stop the marauding vandels invading from Europe or more likely to stop the continual flooding of Walton Village, as the sea would have done for centuries as much of the village remained at sea level.

It is known that there was a Community of people on the Coast at the

11

Naze around the year 1000 AD 'renowned for their Oysters and Cockles', and, at a place which Morant in the 1760's named as 'Waltone'. There could have been a town by the Sea which subsided into oblivion before the Domesday Book was written, and which may have used this spelling. Whether this place had a Wall is unknown, for nothing is recorded from these early times, other than the knowledge that, if it had cockles, then it had to have sandy beaches, and large expanses of sand did exist within the surrounds in the 12th Century.

There have been various suggestions as to Waltons origins, including that repeated in most recent reference books as it being derived from the Danish 'Weala Tun' meaning a 'Farm of the British or Serfs'.

It is a consideration, but 'Weala Tun' does leave the question as to why there are not fifty Walton's or a hundred along this Coastline, for everywhere the Danes struck, there were 'Weala Tun's', or 'Farms of the British', and above all else it must be understood, for centuries, other than for a short period, when the Danes took over this part of the country, generally prior to this time, and later, when they attacked and ravaged the countryside they were not representing Denmark as if it were the Eurovision Song Contest, but they were often a small group of long boats from one of the many communities on their Coastline. Accordingly, an attack on Walton could have been taking place at the same time as another force of Danish Vikings were ransaking somewhere else further along the Coast, and without either being aware of another group making the journey, and it produces the query again as to why there would only be one 'Weala Tun' and not many?

What other choices were there? 'Wealh Tun' or a place inhabited by strangers or foreigners? Was the area of Walton overrun by the Danes, or the Jutes or the Angles, who came, and for a time stayed, using the Village as their base, and it was named with this title?.

With so many flints and arrowheads spread over the Naze, was it called by the Danes 'Weal Tun'. A place of Slaughter? Whilst battles may have raged in and around Walton during the days before History was recorded, just seeing the flints may have produced the name 'Weal Tun'.

Again, did the Romans push a pocket of the natives of Britain, into this part of the Country, and because those that lived and settled were the early

12

Britains, or, as they were known, the Celts, it was to be called in the language of the time, the 'Walh Ton' Was the original name just one of these, and it became rationalised after a Whale was beached in 1329 and the flesh and Oil were distributed to the locals, and the Tongue given to the Bishop of London, and it became, and remained known as the 'Whale Town'.

The origin of the name Walton is therefore quite unknown, and it is as easy to select any one of the above, and use it, for they are all as logical as any other.

The NAZE is also a good indication of utalising guesswork, by selecting what sounds a reasonable idea and using it. The area Eadulvesnaesa was passed to St. Pauls. When historians centuries later started examining the background, they latched onto the 'naesa' part of the name and indicated that, as this meant a 'promontary' in Danish, from then on, this became recognised as the 'true' reason for it becoming 'The Naze'.

The fact that the Romans were here earlier and that they could have stated the land sticking out was a 'Nasa' or a Nose, and as the Saxons and the Danes came in, so the locals repeated the Roman name, and it remained. It could have been any one of a number of attackers that created this name, yet over the years it was to change and it was known as Naisse, Naese and in 1546 as Nayse. In 1329 it had been used as 'Nasse by Waleton'

Recent 'origin of name' books state the obvious because the 'naesa' part fits perfectly, and therefore it 'has to be correct', although writers fail to note other places within the same period which also had a 'naesa' at the end of their names. Wrabnaesa (Wrabness) is an example of a place with no promontary. Accordingly this suggests that the usage of the word 'Naesa' where the Naze is concerned, is one of pure speculation simply because it happens to 'fit the bill'.

There was still a farming village some miles inland during these times, and which eventually has become the Town we know as Walton, but a place on the Coast, pre-1086 is known to have existed, but whether it was ever given a name is another matter. This small place could also have been called Walton. In Frinton there were two Manors with different spellings, and therefore who is to say Walton wasn't the same? In fact this fishing community on the waters edge was probably only a small number of shacks or cottages without any name, and lived in by people within the 'area' of Walton (the Estate), who moved their properties back every fifty or sixty years to new positions, as the land eroded away, and they had to build new homes for themselves and their families.

It has also been suggested that if it had a name it could have been called 'Consumpta' (in Waltone), as there are two stalls in St. Pauls named 'Prebenda of Sneating' and 'Prebenda of Consumpta per Mare' (Consumpta by the Sea) and both are definitely linked with this area, as they also were given to St. Pauls (Prebanda means 'places given') and therefore a place named Consumpta must have existed, for no one would give something to St. Pauls that didn't exist, or had already gone to the waves

Fire has twice (three times if including a second fire after rebuilding was started during the 1090's) destroyed the Church of St. Pauls, and with it went thousands of Manuscripts, including many dealing with Eadulvesnaesa and creating a situation whereby there are now very few documents that can be checked to verify or confirm any of this.

It is also definite that this place, which disappeared at least a thousand years ago, was a fishing 'Community'. It could also, as has been suggested, have been a very small village with a wall surrounding it (or a barrier) to stop the Sea from flooding, making it a 'Walled Town'. On some maps during Morants time, Walton is shown as part of the Sokens and quoted as 'Walton Le Soken' but it was also known as being 'Walton 'in' the Naze' or 'Walton 'at' the Naze', and as the Sea got closer to the Town this changed to that which we now know today as 'Walton 'on' the Naze', and on one map as 'Walton under the Naze'.

KIRBY and the places attached to it, also were altered and written differently. Kyrke (meaning a Church) or Kirkebi, when the name was linked 'iuxta Thorpe' and the 'bi' meaning 'By', or together 'By the Church'.

In 1181 it was called Kirkeley, and then Kerkeby and Kirkbye Soca in the 1400 and 1500's, although by 1535 it was being spelt in some documents as it is today. Maps during the 16th and 17th Centuries were to utalise different spellings as well. Kirby Cross as a name did not appear on maps until the 1800's, so it's origins are clouded and unknown.

14

Included within the lands of Kirby, is BIRCH HALL, which was called Birchou in 1086 (Domesday Book). Bilcho in 1212, and went through Bircho, Biliche, Birchho, Birchhowe, Birchoowe and Birchehall by 1540. Birch Hall lands were under the jurisdiction of St. Pauls for a period, but they rented these out, and they were never part of the 'Sokens'.

In 1222 St. Pauls arranged a survey of the land they owned, and this visitation listed every adult male on their property. This shows the Estate of Walton, Thorpe and Kirby as one area, and then in this visitation, there is also another holding named 'Kirby with Horlock'. Horlock is a mystery and means little. This name has been found on this one document and one later, and various suggestions as to it's origin have been made, including that it is the original name for the area of Kirby Cross, but this is doubtful.

K.D. Crook a diligent historian suggests that Horlock was a large section of land between Kirby and Walton, and elsewhere it was suggested that Horlock's lands were an area owned by someone of this name, and whilst a Thomas Horlock did live within the area in 1458, prior to this, this name does not appear in any visitations, nor does this family name appear within the community later.

Yet the answer may be far more simple. Birch Hall, which is a Manor of Kirby, was for centuries linked with Horsey. It was not part of Eadulvesnaesa and therefore not included within any of the joint write-ups by St. Pauls, but always listed seperately. Birch Hall is not mentioned within the 1222 document and therefore it's logical that Kirby with Horlock is in fact Birch Hall with Horsey.

The various Islands that now exist in the North of Kirby and Walton were originally all joined together with just a few streams and rivers dividing them. (see map at Frontis). On previous visitations in addition to the Manor of Birch Hall, a further area of land, unnamed, was indicated, and which was 7 Hides in size, and this goes in line with the place named in 1222 as being Horlock. This has the strongest possibility of being the area that would have been in existance known today as Horsey and the other Islands. It is believed a scribe or Monk simply wrote in error, as happened quite often in those far off times, when giving the names of places, and he wrote HORLOCK when he had simply left out the letter 's' in what should have been HORSLOC which is a Saxon word for a Horse Enclosure

HORSEY ISLAND has been classified as a Horse Enclosure for centuries and this gives added impetus to the suggestion that it should have been written as HORSLOC in the 1222 document. It should also be noted that neither HORLOCK nor HORLOC means anything in translation, which was not normal for many of the early place names at this time. Once again, the origin might be quite different but as the Islands parted from the land mass, and diminished in size, one retained the name Horsehey or Horsheia and by 1594 as the streams and rivers widened, it became known as Orsey Ilande. Horsey was, prior to the 1400's an important section of the area of Kirby.

SKIPPERS Island was once Holmes Island, but when John Skipper owned it, the name changed and it has remained as such ever since.

SNEATING HALL was possibly the home of Simon de Sneating, and the name appeared as Snetying, Snetiung, Snotyng, Sneddon Hall, Sneddan and even Sniting Hall as late as 1805

GREAT HOLLAND, is another place with a problematic background, for no clear record shows how the name came about. Holanda is mentioned about the year 900 AD and then repeated as two areas within the Domesday Book, and later as a single unit it became known as Hoylande, with the 'e' added, and then without, by 1218. It was Holend in 1440. Great Heyland in 1362, and it was known as 'moche Halland' in 1552. Holland in the Netherlands derives it's name from being a 'Marsh or Hollow land' of which much of Holland in Essex was at the time.

FRINTON is a modern Town, yet as an area, it's name, like those above, was to change and alter with errors made by people copying the name in manuscripts, or pronunceations altering the written word. In 1086 at the time of the Domesday Book, it was to be known as two Manors, Freituna and Frientunam.

The Saxon links here appear paramount, and Peter Boyden suggests that Frinton is from Fritha Tun, indicating someone named Fritha having a Farm there. There is a link with a Saxon warrior named 'Frithu' in the sixth century. Yet the origin of the name could as easilly have been Frige Tun, as Frige is the Saxon God of joy and fruitfulness

There was, from then, until 1500, at least eleven different spellings of Frinton recorded, with Frichintona and Frempton amongst them. At some point there was a link of the name Frinton with the name Skyrmans Fee (in

16

some places written as Skirmans Fee). It has been suggested that this could have been land that was owned by a 'Shireman' or official of the County, yet no further details have come to light to substantiate this.

In 1601 'the Manor of Skyrmans Fee or Frinton Hall' is mentioned, suggesting that the Frinton Hall lands at that time were also known as Skyrmans Fee, but after this reference and another 150 years later, from then on it appears to have been no longer been used. What or who Skyrman Fee was, is now unknown. Various Frinton Halls fell to the on going Sea over the centuries, with the last to go this way in 1720, yet whether any of these earlier Halls were on Skyrman Fee land is unknown, for this land is now way out to Sea.

A breakdown of the various Manors and owners that existed between the year 1000 and 1768 appears in Chapter 15, which shows Morants Lists in some detail.

In the earliest days, Roads and Streets seldom were given names. More so in the period before a proper Postal Service, yet where names were given, there have still been changes, and these include Stewarts or Stuarts Lane which became Elm Tree Avenue in Frinton. At one time it had a fine display of Elms that went from one end of the Avenue to the other, but it wasn't just Dutch Elm that destroyed them, but road widening by the local Council, which got rid of them all.

Witton Wood Road was a smugglers route from the Coast between Kirby and Frinton, which went through Whytton Wood as early as 1552. The name of the road had changes from being called Whitton Lane to that of Whitney Grove at one point.

There was a single unnamed road that ran from Frinton Gates to the Sea, but with the erection of the Railway Station in 1888, it was to become known as Station Road. In 1904, when the Duke of Connaught was staying at the Grand Hotel in Frinton, he agreed to his wife officiating at it's change of name to Connaught Avenue.

Thankfully we have no Mandela nor any political names thrust upon us, which, as the years progress, future generations query their relativity, as the peoples importance fades from memory. How many in Clacton are aware that Peter Bruff Avenue represents the godfather of the Town (as he was for Walton as well) and has nothing to do with Peter Brough (different spelling)

17

a well known ventriloquist, who appeared in Clacton on many occasions, with his wooden friend, Archie Andrews, and was heard on the BBC in nearly every home during the 1950`s

Chapter 2 THE EARLIEST YEARS

In the beginning.........

It would be wonderful to time travel back ten thousand or even 100,000 years just to see what life was really like in those distant days. We know that the earliest Prehistoric creatures had already gone about 500,000 years earlier, and we are aware they roamed around most of Britain.Yet sorting out fact from fiction, based on a period so long ago, is thwart with problems, for it is very difficult to depict an age before documents or manuscripts were written, and then ascertain whether modern writers statements about the time zone are correct or just guesswork.

It was in 1871 that the first thesis of any importance was written about Red Crag, a material found beneath the ground at the Naze. From then on a number of articles have been written and expound on how the Naze shows clearly the basic geological strata from a Pre-Glacial period. Accordingly this is why it was designated by a small group of geologists as being a 'Site of Special Scientific Interest'. Again guesswork becomes paramount in ascertaining when this all took place, but it is a period of anything between ten to fifty million years ago.

The erosion around the Naze has continually produced fossils and bones and by 1877 it had been recorded that over 300 examples had been found, although it is known that over the years many people visiting Walton took home 'fossil' souvenirs without logging them anywhere, so 300 is a very nominal figure, especially when it was stated by John Hanson in 1805 that, whilst 'picnicking on the beaches at the Naze there were the bones of creatures long gone, strewn everywhere'. Of the items found and recorded, there was, in 1803, a thirty foot skeleton of a Mammoth discovered. In addition there have been three different species of Woolly Rhino, The Great Elk, The Straight Tusked Elephant, and many other creatures transcribing a

18

period of at least 200,000 years who lived around the area.

Over l0,000 years ago these animals had changed in type, and were to slowly disappear, and man changed from the hairy to getting closer to that which we are today. Flints in abundance have turned up all around the Naze. Yet what is not understood is that the rock formation used to make these tools, is similar in structure to that found only in Cornwall. Was our ancestor a trader, or were there deposits of flint within the many miles of land that have eroded into the Sea? Until an area at least thirty miles out is fully dredged and examined, this will remain a complete mystery, although, with so many Stone Age tools and impliments it would suggest that there had been deposits for making these, within the Naze, at least 5000years ago.

A few bones of ancient man have turned up, and in April 1911 the complete skeleton of a 25 to 30 year old woman was found, wrapped in grass, in a shallow grave. She was aged about four thousand years old. There were no artifacts in the grave, and the reason for her death is unknown. There are large gaps in our knowledge. We can surmise and expound on what we believe took place during these times, based on similar occurances elsewhere, but there are still large and lengthy periods when nothing is known. The Vikings from Norway were raiding the North of England, and occasionally getting down this way, whilst the Danish Vikings concentrated on the East Coast.

Amongst the raiders/attackers, came the Romans, and the link with Colchester and the Romans are known. Roman remains have been found within the area of Walton, Kirby, Gt. Holland and Frinton. Potsherds. Walls. A site of a Roman Villa but there would have been far more. Erosion has taken it's toll.

A material known as Septaria, was being found along these Beaches, which, when pounded and fired, produced a form of cement which was to be used within the construction of the Roman Walls at Colchester and possibly within the original Castle, but it is also found in the Temple of Claudia. This product is known as Roman Cement, and some of the Septaria used at Colchester very probably originated from Frinton or Walton. When the Romans left, there was a gap of some five hundred years, when the Saxons did little, but the Normans in re-building

Colchester, utalised the materials the Romans had left behind, including Roman foundations, brickwork and Septaria. Then for a further hundred years the product was to be reused, and a small amount can be found in the rebuilt Castle at present, but it is also found within the walls of St. Botolphs Priory (cl095).

In the 1790's this product was re-examined, and James Parker decided to patent the process (although it had been known for so long) and for the next sixty years it was being dredged in quantity along this coastline and shipped to a works in Harwich where they reproduced many of the original methods the Romans had used centuries earlier. This product was to become known as Parkers (Roman) Cement. This continued until Portland Cement was found to have far better properties, During Roman times, it is possible that Walton or Frinton had it's own small kilns along the Coastline to provide the Romans with what they required.

The Romans were to leave. More skirmishes with the Vikings, both the Danes and the Norwegians, as well as the Angles and the Jutes, and it was the Saxons, who came, conquered and were then to rule for over five centuries.

The Naze as we see it today, did not stick upwards like a thumb above the Village of Walton even a few hundred years ago, but it stuck out into the Sea like a nose. To get an even better idea of the Coastline from Clacton to Frinton about the year 1000, add at least five miles out to sea.

To fully understand the Naze, look at the maps in the foreward of this book. With this in mind, use a modern map, and place a marker on the Walton of today and then, at the same scale as the map, mark a distance heading towards the Netherlands and into the Sea at least fifteen to twenty miles. It can be estimated that this was the distance that Walton, the town we know today was from the Coast at least two thousand years ago. It has been suggested that because of it's structure every hundred years between half to three quarters of a mile of the Naze is eroded away, although, during a very low tide in 1878, rubble from buildings were found from a time and period of at least eight hundred years earlier.

What did this Coast look like over two thousand years ago? We shall never know and can only assume specifics based on the present erosion rate, and the shape that we know existed in the late 1500's/early 1600's.

20

Holland in Essex prior to the year 919 AD was owned by Sprowe. It is stated that King Arthurs daughter Aedgyvu or Eadgifu purchased it for Twenty pounds. This was 5 Hides in size. After she had become the third wife of King Edward the Elder, she willed the Holland lands in 961 to her fourth daughter Aelftryth who was to marry King Edgar, yet the story becomes problematic when another source suggests that someone named Aelfgifu could have been involved, a Kinswoman to whom Edgar gave lands at about the same time. Lack of documents ensure this is a very confusing period

The Church was considered an important key within the lives of the various dignitary's and leaders, and King Edgar, with his wifes permission, gave the lands to St. Aedeldryda, the Monastry of Ely, and based on the people involved, the Abbott of Ely, Brihtnoth, and the Bishop of Ely, Aedelwold, this took place sometime between 970 and 981. Within a short time St Pauls in London got to hear of this. They approached the Monks, and suggested that, as they had land at Milton near Cambridge, (known also as Milddeltune) that the Monks, and St. Pauls do an exchange, and topped the suggestion off by offering to pay any outlay or losses incurred, both then and in the future, as the value in men and animals was greater regarding the Holland Lands. The Monks agreed, and so St. Pauls took over Holland for a few years. At that time St. Pauls owned a massive series of Estates which included not only those within Walton, Kirby and Thorpe, but also many others further West and in the South of Essex.

Whatever the reason, within a short time, they then decided after twenty years of ownership to sell off the Holland Lands. This was possibly because they had found it was unlike the other land they owned in the area, as it was mostly Marshland and not just arable. During these few years it had become known a a place with a special 'Jurisdiction' although it was never a 'Soken'

The new owner is believed to have been Bergmund and then by 1086, Lefstan. Lefstan was to split Holland when he parted with half of it to Ingelric, retaining what appears to have been Great Holland.

St. Pauls owned a lot of land, and the area called Eadulvesnaesa, it is believed was possibly given by King Athelston to St. Pauls, around the years 931/940 AD. There is now some doubt as to what exactly took place, as it appears these are part of a group of documents that were produced, or created a number of years after the originals, which St, Pauls had in their possesion prior to the Norman Conquest. These new manuscripts were produced to show how St. Pauls obtained these lands. Yet as the original document no longer exists, there is no way of establishing whether someone, be it Bishop or Monk, had not produced or created a document because masses of original manuscripts had been burnt around the year 1087 AD when the fire that completly destroyed St. Pauls, left little standing and it would have been deemed very necassary to reproduce (rewrite) anything that was considered important, for future usage.

The 'new' documents would have been based on the memories of the Monks and Scribes as to what the originals contained as the majority were written before they were born. Few may not have been looked at for decades and with many hundreds to be rewritten, there would have been errors, both in what was being stated, and also in the actual definition of specifics, yet, who would argue with the Church of St. Pauls if they produced an undated document/manuscript which had been written many hundred years after the originals?

There is no way that we can now be aware why these lands were given to St. Pauls in the first place? It was possibly by some person or individual wishing to keep in with the Bishop of London, as St Pauls had an ear to Rome. It could have been King Athelstan; although early write-ups suggest he was only acting as a middleman on behalf of the person providing the lands. Yet the truth will now never be known.

In 1666 St. Pauls became a victim of the Great Fire of London, and again, much was destroyed. What is known is the knowledge that because of the lands ownership, Eadulvesnaesa was acknowledged by the Saxons as being within a peculiar situation, and, for six hundred years, and until Henry Vlll changed the understanding of the Church throughout the country, the three Parishes (or manors) were to be known as a SOKEN. It must be indicated that this was not the only Soken in the Country, as there were many others

Those living within a Soken held privaleges that provided them with dispensations within their boundries. Women who had land when they married, normally found it automatically became the ownership of the husband, yet, within a Soken, wives were to have joint rights to the

22

property their husbands owned. Those within the Sokens could, with the Churches approval, create their own laws and bye laws.

Some Sokens were as large as that of Eadulvasnaesa and others were very small, and these were spread all over Britain.

Within a Soken you could knock your house down without asking permission. No arrest could be made on Soken land without the Sokens Baliff being present.

All of these original privaleges were agreed by King William in the late 1000's, and succeeding Royalty confirmed their continuation.

As Kirby was in the centre of the three Estates given to St. Pauls, it was here that regular meetings and Courts were to be held, yet Kirby was really only involved in Farming as oppossed to Thorpe, which was a thriving jostling community where the Solicitors, Doctors and other noteworthy's lived. After the lands were taken away from St. Pauls by the Crown in the 1550's, the Church continued to utalise Kirby as a centre, although the resident Vicar was to live and use Thorpe as his main living.

Over the centuries there were occasional problems regarding the Estate. A few years after the 'forged' document had been produced, some of Waltons woodlands were claimed by Richard, Bishop of London, as part of his lands at Clakentona or Clakinton (Clacton). He had to return them when the 'error' was pointed out to him by the legal authorities in 1127.

At face value this seems to be a strange event as no Eadulvasnaesa lands at that time bordered onto any of the lands owned by Richard.

The query has to be whether he truthfully did take these lands or not, as he would have been well aware that they were owned by St. Pauls. This whole matter examined eight hundred years later creates a big question mark. Looking at the circumstances, could this have simply been a 'put up job', concocted by St. Pauls and their Bishop as a way to 'legally' authenticate the Manuscript that they had 'produced' only a short while earlier?

With this being examined and discussed in a court, and using it to make a 'legal' decision, ensured that it's acceptance was guaranteed, and at no time, from then on, would anyone be able to query this Manuscript or what it contained.

It took eight centuries to pass before the first qustion mark was made about it`s validity and the true origins of this document. It was then to become apparent that it had been written in the same hand as a number of other documents and covering a three hundred year period.

Nearly everything held by the St. Pauls Archive has been examined, and it has been found that there were/are a number of other 'fakes' produced during the same period, which appears to have been around the year 1100.

Additional information regarding this era can be found in 'Addendum' at the rear of the book.

Chapter 3   800 YEARS FROM DOMESDAY

The Domesday Book became official in the year 1086 and William, the Norman King then had at his fingertips a record of the country of Britain, which informed him of all that he ruled. He set about building Churches and keeping in with the Church of Rome. Westminster Abbey was to start it's rise within a year of the Conquest (1067) and other Abbeys and Churches owe their beginnings to him.

There are few local Documents during these early centuries that have survived. In 1049 a Danish Viking raider returned to his homeland carrying women and booty from his sacking of Walton, to be struck by a giant wave and they all drowned. In 1190 two fossilised 'teeth' were found in Walton, and considered to be from a 'certain Giant'. It has been stated that these could have been Mammoths Tusks, and yet, based on the size described, they were more likely to be a pair of Rhino Horns as they were recorded as each being the size of two hundred human teeth. As man at that time had never seen either an Elephant or a Rhino, they could not suggest anything closer than their looking like 'teeth'.

Eadulvesnaesa or Aedulvanasa was classified as one Estate in Domesday and consisted in 1086 of having 9 acres of woodland, 300 pigs, 2 Mills, three Salt Pans, and amongst other animals and buildings, 4 Beehives.

In Frinton, the numbers living in the Saxon period were about 10 or more families but by 1670 this was reduced to four and by 1723 it was five families. Frinton was small and just a hamlet with never more than two or

24

three cottages, two Houses and a Church until the 1880's. Basically the whole area of Walton, Kirby, Gt. Holland and Frinton was like an outpost. Too far to get too, and nothing to ensure people stayed when they arrived. Families of workers and farmhands remained. Some of their masters were generous and good, others were not. The land along the coast slipped away.

Over the centuries whilst a lot of things were to happen in Britain, much of the land around Kirby and Walton was to remain quiet under the jurisdiction of St. Pauls. Little changed in either Frinton or Gt. Holland.

It has been suggested that in these early times there had been a Harbour at Walton as the Bishop of London kept his Boat very near to this Coastline, and in those far off days, there may, during erosion and land slippage, have been a natural Harbour at times, but, it must also be understood that, with the area being a Soken, it had to supply sufficient men to sail the Bishop of St. Pauls Boat whenever he needed it, and as such, this crew cost him nothing to be on standby all the time. He therefore moored his boat close to where the men lived who would sail it.

It is known that the Archbishop of Canterbury had to flee Britain in 1052. Joined by Ulf of Dorchester, they rode to Eadulf's Ness (Walton on the Naze) to make their escape. Possibly they went to Walton because they knew it to be small and they were aware the Bishop of London had his Boat there, and surmised it was a small port. They found only one shattered Fishing Boat which they could use, and in it they managed to sail for Normandy. Had this been a viable Port or Harbour, then there would have been far more Boats available than one in a bad state of repair and falling to pieces.

In Gt. Holland nearly five hundred years later, the Manor House was to be used by Anne Boleyn's father in 1545, and later that century, over a twenty year period, the following short list indicates the type of problems that were common all over the country during Tudor times:

Ten Wayes of Cheese were stolen in 1571 in Gt. Holland from John Tendering. They were worth £17 and weighed between 224 and 250 pounds. On the same day, elsewhere in the area, 12 men, many from Kirby, were involved in skirmishes and fighting

25

In 1588 Thomas Markaunt of Great Holland was robbed at his home of £140; two Gold rings; and a silver Salt Cellar. Five months later two of the same thieves returned again, and stole 17 shillings, a hat and some Milan Cloth, but this time they were both caught, and the third member were all hung.

In March 1580 William Clarke was severely whipped because he stole goods to the value of 10 pence halfpenny

An Inquisition was held in May 1583. Petronelle Richard, a servant girl, had, on April 9th, placed within a pig pen, her new born child in order to deface it. It was suggested she had done this because it was still born or dead after arrival as she had not sought the assistance of a midwife.

In the 1650's the people refused to pay their rates, and, because the constables were unable to collect them, the three village constables were fined up to £400 each for not doing their duty. The rates were collected one way or another.

In Kirby they had a hanging tree and a stocks. In Walton, there were also stocks and a Gibbet (scaffold) within the area of Newgate Street. It is believed that this street received it's name after the infamous Prison in London. It was stated in 1335 that the 'Gallows, pillory and tumbrill were kept in the usual places' at Walton.

In both Kirby and Walton they had a Cage which housed prisoners whilst they were awaiting transportation to Thorpe, Colchester, and then to Chelmsford, to stand trial. The Cage in Kirby was at the junction of Halstead Road and Lower Street, and this remained known as Cage Corner for many years. The Cage in Walton was shifted to Walton Hall after it had stood in the centre of Walton for over two hundred years.

Although many people were poor in Elizabethan times, not everyone was, and in Walton when John Broke died in 1582, he left his widow £1000. About £200,000 in 1990's money, yet most people were earning less than a shilling each week (5p)

Occasional disputes were mentioned in Ecclesiastical documents, although they appear minor today, whereby in 1603 Goodwife Keeble punched Mistress Woody in the arm, because she had sat in her pew in Church. Dorothy Richmond in 1593 thrust a pin into the buttocks of Edy Alefounders, during divine service, which created a 'great disquietness'

26

Both happened within Gt. Holland Church.

In 1650 Parliment suggested that Frinton should be amalgamated into the Estate of Walton. This was rejected.

A wreck at Frinton was claimed by St. Pauls in London in 1273. It had been washed up on the beaches. Many considered in those days that Frinton was also part of the Sokens. The Rector at Frinton was Ruffus, who was a Canon of St. Pauls, and therefore maybe it was he that tried to ensure that St. Pauls had the bounty from the wreck. When examined, the Courts stated that the lands were not owned by St. Pauls, and the wreck was definitely not theirs.

For many years, ship wrecks were recorded, because they were officially the joint ownership of the Lord of the Manor and the finder. When the Stuarts came to the throne, this arrangement was altered and it became official that the Lord of the Manor could take everything, and wrecks were seldom recorded (or listed) from that time onwards. Always there have been people who, in all weathers, would risk their lives to grab what they could from distressed shipping, but, after the Stuarts declaration, and knowing how some Lords of the Manor would give them little in return for their efforts, many wrecks were never disclosed to anyone, least of all the Lord of the Manor.

Warren, a Wapping Mariner bought Frinton Hall in 1685, and set about going after wrecks. He was also involved in searching for wrecks under the Sea, especially when he made his name wearing a watertight leather case, attached to a leather pipe with Bellows. The earliest form of Diving Suit, and highly dangerous, which was invented in the early 1700's, and was the cause of his death. It would appear he was uneducated as he could only sign his name with an X. His daughter Joan was betrothed to Capt. James Bushnell, who also went after wrecks. He was Lord of the Manor at both Great Holland and Frinton. He eventually became Lord Chancellor. A man who enjoyed his food, and although five foot eleven, he was six feet around his stomach at that time he was caught in a massive Tidal Wave and drowned. He was buried besides the Porch at Frinton Church in 1738.

Few of the Lords of the Manor lived locally. Their main homes were usually in other parts of the Country. Lord D'Arcy, who owned vast Estates, lived in St. Osyth. In Kirby, Birch House was classified as a 'house of recreation' and used only as a hunting lodge by Theyre of Elderton in 1594. Bishop Burnel acquired the Manor of Gt. Holland when he was also the Bishop of Bath and West and Lord Chancellor, and was to own at one time, 82 Manors in 19 different counties.

In 1551 King Edward VI passed the ownership of the Manors of Walton and Kirby (with that of Thorpe) to Thomas Lord D'Arcy, adding to those he already had, but this was all part of the action in breaking down the stronghold of various Churches, by removing the lands they owned. In 1553, Queen Mary annexed the three Parishes (the Churches) to the jurisdiction of the Bishop of London, as it had been when under St. Pauls ownership, so ecclesiastically things at face level remained the same. Now all Parish Churches in Essex come within the Diocese of Chelmsford (from the 1900's). Not everything though was wine and roses for the Clergy during the changes in the 1500's, especially with the conflicts that arose, and which were to effect and attempt to change belief over the following 100 years.

In 1556 the Rev. Edmund Alabaster whose parishes included Gt. Glacton, Gt. Holland and Frinton was burnt at the stake because he refused to obey the Crown. He was still preaching in June 1555 the older, and then no longer acceptable, English Church Service. Henry VIII had decreed that all Churches sever their links with the Church of Rome, and he, Henry, became the leader of the Church in England, which allowed him to divorce or behead wives as he pleased. Yet during, and even after he died, some Vicars broke what had become the 'new' law. Although reprimanded, Alabaster continued defying the Crown, and he was put to the stake at the same time as were six others from other parts of the Country, who had also committed the same offence.

In Kirby during the early part of the same year, Rev. Thomas Whittall was sent to the stake as well, but here it was all part of the rapid changes between the country becoming Protestant, and then Catholic and reverting to being Protestant again. Many clergy suffered because of this.

Thomas Elmot (or Elinot) in 1572 was teaching his parishoners in Gt. Holland that 'after evening prayer on a Sunday it is lawful to return to work. That the Holy Days appointed should be taken away, for they are idolrous and superstitious. That on 'All Saints Day', it is lawful to go to

28

work all day'. Accordingly he was called before an Archdeacons Court.

Eighty years later Edward Cherry the Rector of Gt. Hollan was classified by the Puritans as a 'Scandalous and Malignant Priest' because 'He usually bowed twelve times to the East when going into the Chancel, and his Sermons were less than one a month which usually upheld superstitous innovations. He also had refused to give Sacrement to those of his parishoners that would not come to the rails to receive it. He taught in his sermons that Baptism washed away original sin. He was often drunk, and he did affirm that a man may more lawfully play, game or drink in an Ale House on a Sunday than on any other day. Further he had published a scandelous libel about the Earls of Essex, Warwick and Holland. He also affirmed he never knew of anything good that Parliment did unless it was to rob the Country, and that he had taken himself to the Army raised against Parliment'.

All of these ensured he was a wanted man, and he had to disappear and he fled to St. Osyth under the sanctuary afforded to him by Lord D'Arcy, but this meant that until Charles the Second became King, he had to take on another identity.

In Walton there had been a wooden Cross that had stood in the centre of the village since the 1100's. What happened to it is unknown, although it was there in 1720. Every July 2nd they held a two day Toy fair, where dancing, drinking and merryment took place. This Fair was eventually stopped in the 1860's after many centuries, although no reasons are given as to why this happened. Kirby had a Fair on Ship Meadow on St. Annes Day, July 27th, and another in August, with the latter being involved in the sale of lambs. Great Holland had a Fair on 22nd June. Frinton had nothing!

There had been for centuries a number of Kirby Halls, but over the years they fell down, and one built in 1556 was replaced by another which was erected in 1750. Walton Hall was to change and alter. In 1222 there had been a group of long buildings on the Naze, with 'The old Hall having a Solar, a private room in the top of the building. A fire place and a Gardrobe. A great Kitchen with a Bakehouse and a Brewhouse and a large Oven. There was a Dairy and a large Granery. A Henhouse and a great Stable outside. Also there was a new Cowhouse as the old, which included a Oxhouse and a Stable had begun to fall to the sea. There was a Chapel and a Chamber adjoining with five glazed windows. A dovecote and alongside, a building which held Waggons and Carts, and by the Great Hall Door there was a small cellar'. It is unknown whether the one which was falling down was the same, but at about this time, there had been a huge barn, 160 foot long, on the Naze.

Walton Halls were built and then they were destroyed, either by the encroaching Sea or subsidence on the Naze.

All four Churches had fallen into disrepair during the 1700's. Owing to the lack of money within the four communities, there was never enough to warrant any rebuilding. It is known that smugglers hid their goods within the Churches, and if there was a service, then the contraband was hidden in the roof, guttering, or in Coffins, although it was known that on occasions a cloth was simply hung between the Parishoners and the Bounty at Frinton. It would therefore be naive to suggest that Rectors were unaware of what took place, as many benifited from smugglers using Church property.

In the mid 1700's, because it was cheap, Gin was the 'workers Drink', although not of great quality, and at a time when the population of Britain was less than one tenth of that today, over Five and a Half million gallons of Gin was being drunk annually! Dutch Gin was of a similar quality and as cheap, but as the revenues (Tax) increased in Britain at specific times it became profitable to smuggle it into the country for limited periods.

Often smugglers hauls were found and confiscated. In 1779 34 tubs of Gin were recovered in Kirby, plus a cart and two horses, and a further 86 tubs and some Tea were recovered in Walton. Fifty years earlier in Frinton, a Customs Officer had found buried 19 half ankers of Brandy. A half anker was about five gallons of liquid, and the term was to be changed to Tubs or casks towards the end of that century.

Many smugglers were known to the locals. One named Captain Palmer lived with his daughter Lucy, on a farm in Walton (See Chapter 9).

Between Frinton and Walton there had been a cove named 'Smugglers Gap', but erosion eventually took this away. Locals would usually assist the Smugglers and were passed gin for their efforts. Peter Bains helped when they off-loaded on Gt Hollands beaches in the mid-1700's. He also assisted in changing their Horses, and always he received a tub of Gin, which he liked and drank regularly.

The gangs would travel down Dead Man's Lane from Kirby and into Witton Wood and then to the beaches of Frinton and returning that way en-route to London.

On one occasion Richard Brett of Great Holland was rebuilding the Sea Wall when the smugglers arrived and he and his friends assisted unloading the goods. They were all given a quantity of Gin for their efforts, which they drank until it was finished. On the way home, Brett slipped and fell into a stream when crossing the marshes. His friends had difficulty getting him out as they were also very drunk, and they left him to sober up alongside the water he had fallen in. The next morning they discovered the night had been so cold, he had frozen to death, as his body was still in the same place where they had left it. He left a wife and six children who became dependant on the Parish.

In Walton, in 1840, the schoolmaster would take 2 hundred weight of Tobacco on a pack Horse each Friday evening after the school day had finished, and treck some distance from Inn to Inn and Ale House to Ale House, until he had sold it all, and then return in time to play the organ and teach Sunday School.

It has been rumoured that three pubs, the 'Red Lion' in Kirby, and both 'The Ship' and 'Lions Den' in Great Holland, had smugglers escape tunnels. Whilst there was probably a 'secret' way out of each, it was possibly no more than an ordinary door or a simple latched window, covered with barrels or foliage so it could not be easily seen. As the years progressed and word of mouth altered the truth, these escape routes developed into mythology and grew to become 'escape tunnels'. There were also rumoured Tunnels from a number of houses within Kirby and Gt. Holland, but these also, are all myths promoted by time and extensive enquires indicate that none existed.

Basically smuggling decreased, and as far as is known, vanished after the railways were opened. The reason for this is not known, but no smugglers were caught within the area from the 1860's onwards.

There had been a Customs man at Kirby Quay for many centuries. The layout of the Quay enabled two Barges alongside one another, and six or seven more would be waiting. The advent of the railways ensured the Customs man was no longer needed, and in 1868 he was moved to Walton,

31

because of the growth of Landermere Wharf, and Kirby Quay slowley silted up, although it was still used for many years for Coal deliveries. It eventually left the Granery building on it's own, and which has now been converted into a house. For years, the Quay had been a minor Port, with a Lime Kiln, A counting House. A Lime House. Corn Granery and a Dwelling House. Store House and a Stable and Coal Yard.

By the Quay at Kirby there had been a Windmill, which a gale destroyed in the 1740's. Another windmill stood in the area now known as Kirby Cross, alongside the main road to Thorpe. It was owned for many years by the Wilson family, who had a Farm directly opposite. His house still standing, is now named Willow Farm, instead of it's original name, Wilsons Farm. In Gt Holland, after being rebuilt in 1838, the Windmill there had two set backs. In 1858 it was struck by lightning, and then in 1863 the top of the windmill was completly taken off through hurricane winds, and changed for a short period, to become a steam driven mill. The sails and the roof were repaired, and it returned to being a Windmill, but they retained a 'Donkey' engine as a safeguard should any future problems arise. The Gt. Holland Windmill ceased being used in the 1930's and was burnt down on Christmas Eve 1986.

Walton had two Mills at the turn of the 19th Century, a Windmill and a Tide Mill. It has been suggested that the Tidemill had been working in the 14th Century, yet it's design is considered to have been originally Dutch, and believed to have been constructed at a time when the Dutch were in the area working on land reclamation in the 17th Century. Had a Tidemill been there earlier it would probably have been of a different design, and closer to Stone Point, for there was only a growing river in the 1300's, as oppossed to it even approaching anything like the site which the Yacht Club took over in the 1920's. Both the Tidemill and an earlier Windmill were purchased by John Archer in 1834.

Some write-ups suggest that the Tide Mill had up to nineteen stones grinding away, but this is doubtful, although the actual true size of the building is unknown. It probably had four and maybe as many as six stones working at any one time. The large number of stones suggested is simply the amount that the normal large sacks of flour at that time weighed, which was 19 stones, but with time and lack of knowledge, the usage of the word

32

'stones' has become intermingled and confused.

Barges continually tied up alongside the Tidemill to fill up with the sacks of flour destined for London. The Walton Windmill provided everything for local usage, but it had been in a bad state of repair when it was purchased by Archer and he rebuilt it in 1846. Archer had four of his own barges to ship his flour to London. It was normal for many of them to return with Coal in equally large sacks, and then, using the same Boats with Coal Dust still below decks, to be refilled with more flour sacks as quickly as possible, for the return journey to London.

During all this time, the link with Walton and a Harbour is repeated. In 1567 it was known that there was an 'under' 20 ton vessel moored at Walton, yet this could have been anchored in the Backwaters, or out to sea, and it wasn't until the mid-1700's, the area where the Yacht Club now is, was being called Landermere Wharf, and by 1781 the Wharf was taking on the trappings of becoming a small Port, with not only Grain and Coal being landed, but also Scandinavian Timber being shipped in regularly.

In the 1830's Mr Jeffries was not only the senior Coastguard in Walton, but also the Customs Officer. There had been Coastguards stationed in the area for years, and with their families they were housed from the 1830's in the Martello Tower still standing. Conditions there were bleak and very bad. They were then transfered to the hulk of a ship named the 'Blossom' moored in the Backwaters, which had no facilities at all, ensuring a walk through mud and filth for every man, woman and child. It was in the late 1880's their plight was established and after the Coastguard building by the original Lifeboat House, was built in 1890, five cottages were created to accomodate them in 1901.

There were Blacksmiths forges in all four areas, although that in Frinton had to change when the premises fell into the Sea, and it moved to a site close to where 1st Avenue is today. In Walton there were, as the Town was to grow, eventually three Brick Kilns, with the earliest attached to Landermere Wharf in 1794. In Frinton, one small Kiln in Pole Barn Lane had been started in about 1880. This was then moved to the end of Witton Wood Road where it's capacity increased ten fold. Kirby had a Brick Kiln by the Quay in 1898.

33

Walton was involved in the production of Ink, a beautiful transparent blue Ink, which, when it had been used for writing on paper or manuscript, it slowly changed from Blue to Black through Oxidisation. This was produced from Copperas mixed in pits with various metalic substances.

When other materials were added to amounts of crushed Copperas, such as Sumac, Fustic, The Bark of Trees, Vitriol, Logwood, Potash etc, it was used to dye cloth and leather. Everything depended on the very long boiling times (in some cases up to seven or eight hours) and the amount of Copperas and the materials being used. The results were most colours, from Yellow to Mulberry, as well as a series of shades of Black (Red Black, Blue Black etc). The Copperas acted as a mordant, for it was used to 'fix the dyes' so they wouldn't wash out or run. It was never used as a colouring agent to produce only Black as the Victoria History of Essex suggests.

There were at one time two works producing the Ink and crushed copperas, but one was destroyed by fire in about 1725 (although some write-ups state it was lost to the Sea) and the other continued until 1855, when Ink production was stopped, although for the next ten years they still crushed Copperas.

Copperas were found on the Coast, and pickers went gathering and despatching by cart or barge to the works in Walton. The men, women and children involved in this, came from Walton, Frinton, and Gt Holland and were paid with 2 pence tokens based on every bushel of Copperas they gathered. These coins were used in the local shops to buy their needs. There was a Copperas Works in Harwich which continually produced Ink after Walton closed. The gathered Copperas were sent there for some years. When Harwich closed, everything was sent to a Works in London but the increasing costs, and with better, cheaper alternatives coming from Asia, eventually even the London works were to close as well.

Some of the land at Kirby was owned by the Honywood family. One lady from this family when she died, aged 94, had 367 direct line living relatives which included Children, Grand Children, Great Grandchildren, and even Great Great Grandchildren.

Religion for many in these small areas was important, even if they sometimes only saw the preacher occasionally, yet, during the 1500's and starting in 1542, a plague of fear went throughout the land, as seeking witches became fair game. Henry Vlll had proclaimed that witches existed. From then until the late 1600's, everyone was listened to who had a grudge, or didn't like a neighbour. Children made comment and soon suspected witches were being sent to prison and awaiting a Trial.

It was initially in St. Osyth where a number were to be tried, when in the mid-1500's Lord D'Arcy, who owned most of St. Osyth, was the main protagonist, where he listened to simple stories told by his serfs, and although being told to him in good faith and confidence, they found themselves, or the people they had named, standing Trial, as D'Arcy passed every detail onto the authorities and even sat in judgement on some of them

By the 1600's, it was the Witchfinder General, Mathew Hopkins of Manningtree (who was eventually buried in Mistley) that sat in judgement of many Witches. He actually tried none of the locals, although Kirby had two, Walton three and Great Holland had seven during this period. Generally they were, in the main, widowed ladies, who were sad, growing old, with sharp tongues, and often having a knowledge of Herbal remedies.

This knowledge ensured they were called upon to assist when anyone was ill. Doctors cost money, and it was established too often in those early days, they were not always able to help, with many considering blood letting, using leeches, as the only major source of curing all ills, yet, it was the local 'mother' or 'dame' with sympathy and herbs, who could often acheive what appeared to be 'miracles'.

It was this knowledge, that ensured they were automatically suspected by the head hunters, who would find any excuse to put on trial and to hang those considered 'different'. Margery Grewe in Walton was deemed a Witch because she carried a pet Jay on her shoulder which she talked to. How many elderly ladies today would be classified as witches because they have Budgerigars, especially if these birds can talk?

Bridget Mayers of 'Much Holland' (Gt. Holland) indicates the bizarre considerations and ideas of the time. She had two Mice and a Frog. She kept these as pets. The Mice were called 'Jack' and 'Prickeare', and the Frogs name was 'Robin'.

According to the evidence against her she sent the Frog to kill three children. She also had a pet Sparrow, which was sent to kill another child.

35

The reason for these 'murders', it was stated by her accussers, was that she had 'done so because she had been refused milk', and other such reasons. She went on trial twice, found guilty and hung.

These Ladies were on an 'if you win, you lose' situation. The best way to tell a witch was to tie their big left Toe to their right Thumb, and then throw them into a pond, river or stream. If they floated, they were Witches. If they sunk and drowned, then they were not. Some were unproven, like one of the ladies from Walton, who was tried twice. She was returned to Jail both times then her name disappears from the records, presumably dying before her third appearance. Bewitching people was also evidence of witchcraft and Helen Bretton of Kirby was stated to have done this and was Hung. There were a few men who were tried for witchcraft, but all twelve in this area were women. Throughout the Country one in six were either hung or put to the stake. A few were released, unproven, some had one year sentences, others remained in prison forever.

It has been suggested that there is a Witch buried in Gt Holland Churchyard, but this is doubtful, as the burial is within consecrated ground. This myth was continued over the years because there is a Skull and Crossbones on her tombstone, which for nearly two hundred years locals have indicated she was a witch (or some suggested she was a Pirate), yet a few tombstones pre-1800 had a Skull and crossed bones on them, and then in later years stonemasons turned their attention to producing cherubs, angels or other carvings, and today childrens memorial stones might have a Teddy Bear. The ladies husband is buried close and he died after living to an old age, and the death of the lady is recorded normally and without any additional information within the Burial register at the time.

The rich owned land and property. The Manor of Mistley in the 1770's was owned by the flambouant Rt Hon. Robert Rigby, a member of Parliment and the Paymaster General who bought the Estates of Kirby and Walton (and Thorpe) because he wished to drive all the way from his home in Mistley, to the Sea at Walton, on his own land! He tried to get it all re-amalgamated into one Estate, as it had been under St. Pauls jurisdiction. He did not succeed. He might have died in obscurity, had it not been for a scandal in 1779 to which his name was linked. (See Chapter 9). He owned considerable properties, of which nearly all had to be sold to repay his debts and Death duties. Walton Hall, which as part of his Estates, was believed to have changed ownership on the turn of a card a century earlier, when Lord Rivers lost the Hall playing cards with the Earl of Rochford.

As the centuries passed, life changed, as did the attitudes of the young. The 19th Century brought the first glimmer of hope with Education. It also brought Unions. The Machine age. The rebirth of religion. All four between them, altered men's (and women's) thinking.

The only thing that people knew, and understood, was that if they lived too near the Coast, their homes and their lives were being altered every few years as the waves took away large amounts of land. Daniel Defoe, when visiting Walton in 1722/3 ascertained that over 30 Acres had dropped into the sea within the living memory of the people he spoke to. This would have represented a period of about sixty years. Few could read, and even less could write. To travel even to the next Village was something only small numbers would have done. They were told of the wonders of the big cities, but they had their homes and their work, and their beer, and they required little else. Within thirty years of the new century, in 1830, things began to alter which effected everyone. (See Chapter 5)

The lives of the people had continued the same way for centuries. There were Salt Pans in Kirby and Walton, as Sea Salt was the only way of gathering this needed commodity. There had been a Toll Gate leading into Frinton, but based on the numbers who would have used it, it was there for only for a short period of time.

From before 1594, on the Naze, there was a forty foot tower, which was always considered to have been a Sea or Land Mark. Yet it's height wasn't enough for most shipping, and in 1625 sailors were using the top of Walton Hall as their marker to guide them in or out of Harwich. When Trinity House examined the small Tower in 1700 they found it was in a bad state of repair, with it 'being so ancient and cracked that it could not be built on', and stated 'they did not believe it had been erected as a 'landmark', but had been used for beacons which would have been placed on the top of it'. They built a new Tower during 1720 which was completed in October 1721. Designed by Mr. Ogbourne, it cost £784. The earlier Tower was taken down in 1824 and the rubble used for foundations within Walton.

The new Tower was originally 80 foot high, and then in 1796, a further fourteen foot was added. (See Chapter 14). Both this and the Thatched cottage in Hall Lane, are now the two oldest buildings in Walton. In Frinton only The Wick, still remains from this period. Gt. Holland and Kirby were fortunate in retaining many pre-1800 buildings, with 'The Linnett's' (c.1600) in Kirby Cross still being lived in. Amongst the oldest buildings, other than the Churches in Kirby and Gt. Holland, are the Inns or Public Houses, although they have changed with alterations, both externally and internally.

'The Red Lion', or as it was known in earlier times 'The Lion' at Kirby, dates back to the 14th Century. 'The Ship' in Gt. Holland, was in existance in the 16th Century. The Kirby 'Ship' was originally an Alehouse in one of two cottages. The other cottage was a Ships Chandlers, and it was eventually to be amalgamated into it becoming a Beer House, which grew and changed to become an Inn.

The 'Lions Den' in Gt. Holland has 17th Century links, and was originally known as the 'Lion Inn'. During the 1840's it changed to the 'Red Lion Inn' and during the early part of this century it became the 'Lions Den'. The 'Hare and Hounds' in Kirby, goes back to the 1600's, but where it stands now is neither it's original site nor it's original name. Known as the 'The Swan' it then became known as 'The Seven Ashes'. This was then to change to the 'Hare and Hounds' in the 1800's. In 1927 the place burnt down, and the landlord/owner took over two large Houses some short distance from the old building, and converted them in 1928 into the present 'Hare and Hounds'.

In 1876 the 'Railway Tavern' opened in Kirby Cross, and the name changed to become the 'Railway Hotel' and then the 'Kirby Tavern'. It has been suggested that this had been built on the site of an earlier Ale House 'The Greyhound', but whilst this was situated in Upper Street, it was to be found in a cottage that faced the end Halstead Road. Another Ale House in Kirby Cross had been the 'Fox and Hounds' also in Upper Street.

In Kirby Le-Soken, there had been the 'Royal Oak' which was also an Ale house, and is as such still standing, although during it's heyday only one room was used as the 'Tap room' and the building is now a private residence. Over the centuries there would have been other Ale Houses and Inns.

In Walton there had been the `Falcon Inn` in the 1400`s and the `Dukes Head` during Elizabethan times, and an Ale House known as the `Angel` was recorded during the 1600`s.

Erosion ensured these were all to go to the waves or alter with time, and therefore all the Pubs and Inns now exisiting in Walton are reasonably young with the oldest, being `The Victory` which dates from just after the period when Nelons Boat was involved in fighting the French. It is dates around the 1820`s

Chapter 4   PARISH CHURCHES
and OTHER RELIGIONS

The oldest exisiting Church within the area has always been classified as St. Mary`s of Frinton, because there is recorded a dispute regarding an incoming Rector in 1192. To look at the Church today, and to compare it with statements of yesteryear, it basically hasn't changed greatly in shape from the earliest times, but little of it's fabric, both internally and externally shows any link with the centuries past. It was refurbished in an 'Early English Style' in 1879, and this does have a tendency to hide the truth as to what is now being seen, unless you have expert knowledge.

Basically all three Churches in Kirby, Frinton and Great Holland, have remained on the same sites that they now stand. Frinton was, in 1725, the second smallest Parish Church in Britain, and it is now the smallest in Essex.

In Frinton it is believed that part of the original Saxon floor still remains under the present, and when some flagstones were taken up in the 1800's, there was basically just a thick bed of shingle that was literally quite impossible to break down because it was so hard. There are still two 14th century amorial shields which have been partially restored within one of the side windows. These are suppossed to represent the families of Warenne and Elderbeke according to the Royal Commission on Historical Monuments, yet others believe the Elderbeke emblem is really that of the Baynard family, who carried a similar motive on their shield into Battle, and a Baynard owned Birch Hall in Kirby.

39

Many descriptive works on the Church state that the Nave is 14th Century and the South Porch was added in the 16th Century. Over the following years based on what happened to the Church, little was left standing during and throughout the 17th and 18th Centuries. At one point it is recorded that other than a very small section of the walls and part of the West End of the Church, nothing was left of the building in 1786, and all that was to be seen standing were recorded as being 'remains', and based on the continual alterations that happened over the following years to the Church, it is very doubtful whether anything being seen now is actually pre-1850, other than the repaired Amorial Glass mentioned in one window.

There is a Frinton Parish Register, for 1638 to 1640 still existing as a single page. In 1683 it is known that there was no Bible, Prayer Book, communion Table, and many other things were missing, suggesting the previous outgoing Vicar took everything with him, or they had been stolen.

To indicate the problems and the changes, an understanding of what happened in the early part of the 1700's, and the events that followed, all give the clue as to what we now see is really all mid-19th Century rebuilding.

There was a fierce gale on 25th Nov. 1703, which knocked over the Bell Tower and 'what remained of the Chancel'. This left just part of the walls standing. It was then suggested that the Nave be removed and the materials used to rebuild the Chancel, but instead, the Chancel was taken down and the Nave completly re-built, creating a very small Parish Church, 22 foot by 18 and a half foot.

By 1765, it had reverted back to being in a very derelict state and it was a number of years before any rebuilding took place, and continual deterioration ensued during that time, and it was only in the 1800's when Richard Stone lll (he was the third Richard Stone in line), became Church-warden, that changes were to happen because he took the job very seriously, and it was he that set about the refurbishment that was to happen.

In January 1835 he initially arranged some rebuilding and a degree of patching up. It was during this period that he planted Ivy around the Church, as it was considered a decorative way of covering the walls, and it also had a latitude of movement within it's foliage to stop future storms doing damage by keeping the brickwork together. Initially this decorative

40

greenery ensured that the people who travelled to Walton and those that made the trip for the day from Colchester, would always visit the Church at Frinton because of it's delightful and charming appearance, and it was the Ivy which was to become a fund raiser for many years, as the Church looked pretty and visitors were generous.

As the years progressed, the ivy eventually pushed over the rebuilt Bell Tower, ensuring visitors were to became less impressed with the Church. The Ivy was to creep under the tiles and it started taking them off the roof as well. This created many holes and the sight of buckets and containers on the floor to catch the rain, even during services, ensured people didn't stay long enough to leave anything to the Churches upkeep, and by 1859 it was again in an exceedingly poor condition, with a door that was difficult to move and one single window that could only be slightly opened within the church, which ensured that the building would have been airless if it had not been for the draughts and wind that came through the holes in the roof.

In 1860, although it was noted there were 55 seats, the church members attending on a Sunday were usually no more than 2 or 3 people, and at most six. Forty years later with the growth of the Town, by 1902 they were holding two services every Sunday Morning.

This was a time of change in Church law, whereby in 1869 it was stated 'a man may not marry his own Grandmother'.

The roof was to be repaired twice because of the damage created by the Ivy. In 1868, when more repairs were being done to the Church, Richard Stone attempted to destroy it completly, but it wasn't until 1879, when he arranged for the Church to be completly rebuilt that the Ivy was disposed of forever. In that year the Church acquired a new Porch, new roof, a new East Window, new West Windows and a new Chancel, and further repairs throughout the building were to take place.

In the rear of the Church is a window presented by Peter Bruff, in memory of his mother.

This window had to be removed at one time, for as the town grew, the Church was found to be too small, and a temporary extension to seat an additional two hundred and sixty was added to the previous extensions and rebuilding that had happened in 1835, 1868, 1879 (when it could seat 90); 1894 and the massive extension of a temporary nature was built in 1911 and

41

by so doing, creating seating for nearly 400.

This structure, costing £700, was supposed to last no more than ten years, but firstly the first world war, and then deciding to erect the new Church, ensured it stood for eighteen. From 1912, because of the size and nature of the building it needed three large Coke Ovens to keep it warm.

Prior to the extension being added, an Electrical Company (possibly Reedes and Walters) provided the old Church with a new Bell and a new Electrical system to ring it. This continually broke down and it then had to be rung as other Bells, by hand. They had purchased two Warner Bells after the those they were give were damaged after the Bell Tower was pushed over by the Ivy. One of the Warner Bells was replaced with the Electrical Companies, and this was held in store until the new Church was completed and then rehung there.

The site for a new Church was established in Queens Road. Selected in 1924, the plans were drawn up and a fine model was submitted by Sir Charles Nicholson. This was rejected as being far too grandoise and a simpler design was produced and a new plot of land between Old Road and Fourth Avenue was selected. A vote of 370 to 15 was given as an acceptance to this new site, and the land was presented to the Church by the owner of 'The Wick', G Hutton Potts. A corner stone was laid in 1928 by the wife of the Lord Mayor of London, Sir Charles Batho with a large parade of local groups, including the Scouts and Guides. British Legion etc.

A year later the Church was completed, and consecrated by the Bishop of Chelmsford on the 17th July 1929. Although the new building, had foundations for a Tower, it was decided not to include one in the final structure. In 1930 a new organ made by Cartwright and Sons of London was installed, and the Church Hall was completed by 1932.

The small Church of St Mary's is still used occasionally, and in the 1950's a member of the congregation purchased in auction a window showing 'The Annunciation'. Made by William Morris, and designed by Burne Jones in about 1865 for a completly different church, it fitted perfectly into where the previous windows had been damaged during the war years.

Within the Churchyard is a tombstone to writer Ursula Bloom, whose book 'Rosemary for Frinton' told of her days in the Town. It is apparent that, other than two, there are no stones pre-1900 remaining. This is resultant of the Churchwarden having the rights to the Glebe (lands attached to the Church) and renting it to various farmers whose cattle were allowed to wander too close to the Church to graze, and they knocked over and destroyed all the tombstones. In 1865 there was one monument and three graves, and ten years later it was stated by a visitor that 'there is only one tombstone standing, and this is of recent date'. The Glebe was at one time about 32 acres, but much of this had gone to the Sea by 1880.

Beside the Church for years had been a large Pond, which 'even in the driest times, and during a drought, the Pond was never without water' and it was this that many within Frinton used for their drinking supply before the 1880's, although it was called the 'Horse Pond', indicating that the animals also used it. It was to be filled in during the 1960's, and today there is a block of flats on this site. At the other side of the Church stood Frinton Hall which had been built in 1720. The earlier Hall, had ended up standing at the side of the beach and was demolished during a storm that year. It now rests about half a mile out to sea in line with the Crescent. The new Frinton Hall was lived in until extensive storm damage in 1927 and it had to be demolished during 1930.

The Living of Gt.Holland Church is as old as that at Frinton based on it's early St. Pauls connections. A page of the Parish Registry from 1629 suggests that Gt. Holland was of a reasonable size and over the years, the church would have had alterations and structual work, although, only that started in May 1866 is noted, when Arthur Bloomfield redesigned and rebuilt the church and completly refurbished the outside with stone cladding. This was all paid for by Joynes the Curate, because at the time 'the Church was delapidated and unworthy of the Parish'.

There is a query regarding the Tower, owing to few major works on Medieval Brickwork or Buildings even considering it's age, yet it was built between 1413 and completed by 1420, when it was normal to build no more than 12 feet (about four meters) a year, to allow each new added height to settle, based on the morter being used in those early days, suggesting that the time span is correct, based on the height of the Tower. This date is given at the base of the Mallet that was used four hundred years later, when laying the foundation stone of the 'new Church' in 1865. It has written on it, that the Tower has remained exactly as it had been in 1413/1420. As such, this is a fine example of Medieval Brickwork, although it is known by few.

Outside the Church there are only a few older tombstones, with those from 1819 onwards readable. Much of the time there was no resident Curate, and in one year, during 1817, there were seventeen visiting clergymen taking the services and it was assessed in 1862 that over a third of the Village had never been in the Church in their lives.

Possibly, other than the 1420 Tower, the oldest visual part on what was originally Church property still stands in the garden of the Old Rectory. A Turkey Oak planted in c1714 which is now over 275 years old.

Kirby Church Tower was also known to date from the 13th Century, although nothing of that remains. The original Church had a small square Tower with two Bells in 1297. Three hundred years later, there had been added two more bells, making a total of four, plus a hung Sanctus Bell. At some period during the 16th or early 17th Century, it has been suggested that the Tower was rebuilt, although there are no documents showing this. A fifth Bell, made by Miles Grange of Colchester, was added in 1641, and this still exists today, although the others were all to be replaced in 1729.

Another Bell was added in 1778, making a total of six, but the Sanctus Bell had gone. For centuries they had used handbells to lead processions within the church. The Building itself was completly revamped in the 1750's as the roof, and part of the walls were gone, and it is known the Tower was repaired in 1818.

Although Kirby had been linked with Thorpe and Walton in the period when the lands and living were under St. Pauls jurisdiction, there were few changes when the Churches came under the banner of the Bishop of London in the 1550's, for everything had still to be verified, altered or changed through him, and yet, on the 20th June 1777 Robert Rigby of Mistley stated that the Vicarage House in Thorpe, couldn't be used by the Vicar because it was no more than a cottage, and in which a cottager was already living. He then proposed that the area of Walton, Kirby and Thorpe become linked together as it had done in previous years, and that there be solely one living. The Bishop of London looked into this and the suggestion was rejected.

The church at Kirby had a cross, which had a relic, 'piece of the True Cross' within it, in the 1400's, but when the Church was to be completly rebuilt in 1833, by Joseph Grimes the builder, this Cross had already disappeared.

The new design was typical of the period, whereby, although there were 900 people living in Kirby, only enough pews for 35 labourers/workers were provided at the rear of the building, and over 200 for the gentry and their staff. This was usually because it had been the wealthy of the Parish who provided most of the funds to rebuild, and normally the poor had contributed nothing, and most Vicars in those earlier times relied on their living from the 'richer' members of the Parish they were in. Also it gives greater understanding why 'other' religions were to grow, where class had nothing to do with those attending. When the Church was redesigned by Henry Stone, and then rebuilt in the 1870's a further fifty workers/labourers were provided with seating (making then a total of 85), yet the majority of pews were still for the rich. It was during this time the Kirby Church had strong links with the Foreign Bible Society.

The exact date of the Tower is unknown excepting that it is 15th Century based on the Interior fitments, but externally, it can only be classified as Victorian, for nothing visually remains of the original Tower.

In 1871 it was stated that the Vicar was in poor health and that the Curate was an eccentric. When the Vicar died, it was the Curate, the Rev Coxhead, who replaced him. The living was variable, whereby for one period in the 1500's, seven acres of arable land came with the job, although 400 years earlier, there were '10 good acres', and at that time, within a Soken there were also 'perks', whereby the Vicar could claim the best upper garment of any corpse, when he read the burial service.

Nearly all the monuments within the present Church date from the 1870's. In the Graveyard there are a number of older tombstones. The Stone family were regular members at Kirby, because Richard Stone ll owned Willow Farm, and most of his family, are buried at Kirby. He gave his son, Richard Stone lll £1000 in the 1830's to buy Frinton Hall, which had been rented by the Stone family from the 1780's, and this is why the son and many of 'his' family, were to be buried at Frinton. Richard Stone the fourth, moved to America. He revisited Frinton in the early part of this Century, but now his whereabouts and what happened to him or his family areunknown.

In 1926 the Bells at Kirby became a problem. One was cracked, and the others were losing their tone and with the exception of the bell made in 1641, they were all despatched to Ipswich, where they were re-caste. In that year, through the generosity of an elderly Miss Barron, two more bells made by Alfred Boswell, were given to the Church, which made a complete 'peal' of eight. In 1930 a short ring of 700 changes was made, and one of 600 in 1931. In 1955 the Bells were all (with the exception of the 1641 Bell) recaste again, and then in 1960 they produced a ring of 22,400 changes lasting eleven and three quarter hours and breaking the existing national record.

Walton's original Church is believed to have stood for over five hundred years, but as the town came closer to the Sea, subsidence effected everything, and the Tower on the Church, which was of both wood and stone, collapsed in 1748.

After the Tower fell down, a further building was to be built by the side of the Church to enlarge it. It seems strange, considering the situation, that they should create a building or enlargement to the Church when they were well aware of the effects of erosion and subsidence, but the addition is to be seen in two drawings produced in 1777.

In 1798, after a sermon given by the Rev John Stoney on the 22nd July, during the night, part of the roof collapsed within the Church and from then on the building was considered unsafe.

Only a few years earlier, 'The Dukes Head' and two shops had gone to the waves, and they had been situated close to the Church. All had existed since Elizabethan times, so the locals were well aware, based on centuries of knowledge, what would happen to the Church eventually. They knew that once part of the building went, the rest would follow. Yet it would appear they quite unprepared for it going when it did, as it took six years before a new Church was to be built, after the roof in the old had collapsed.

Over the next seven years, from 1798, Walton Church slowly fell down, although the Porch remained until nearly the last. A few weddings actually were held in the Porch, and one of the Churches original Bells was hung

No other services were held at the Church until the new was completed, with everything being transferred to Kirby during the change over period.

As the building started to fall down, the land surrounding the Church also dispersed and coffins within the original cemetary were being washed up along the beaches. As they were usually empty by the time they returned to the shore, people used the wood for doing jobs around their homes. It was good wood. Coffins were sticking out of the cliffs for years and many were being forced open for the teeth, as there were no false teeth or dentures in those days.

In 1803 some members of the 42nd Regiment of Foot (The Black Watch), stationed at Weeley, were detached to guard the Coastline at Walton. They were found on one occasion, within the remaining walls of the church, using the churches font as a Brazier when trying to keep warm, and also using it to cook on. Within two or three years, the Church walls went completly, and some of the materials from the old Church were used as foundations in building the new.

On the 17th June 1804, the new building was completed, and a month later, on the 17th July, it was consecrated by Beilby Porteus, The Bishop of London. The land for the new Church had been presented to the Church Council by Daniel Brown a local landowner and farmer, but this generous gift ensured that he was also the first to be buried in the new Churchyard, as he died five days after the Church had been sanctified, on the 23rd July 1804. In 1832, and then again in 1835 rebuilding work took place to enlarge the building, and a narrow tower was built alongside in 1838.

Services could only be given to 100 people initially but the new work provided a further 200 seats and a visitor was to make the comment that the Church was 'destitute of Ecclesiastical Character and insufficient to accomodate the number living within the town'. The Graveyard was far too small and just over eighty years later by 1886, it was full, and another site had to be found, for the towns growth ensured it was to be needed.

By 1868 the Church needed extending, and from then until 1882 the Church was altered, rebuilt, and rearranged, but this was over a period of time, as the money was slow to come through. It had been designed by Henry Stone (Richard Stones son) and consecrated in Jan. 1882. In 1896 the

47

existing Tower had been built, and after the Clock had been installed, by 1898 the Church is, as it is seen today.

To raise monies for completing the loan made to rebuild the Church, and assist with funds for the Tower, there was the opportunity in 1892 to sell some of the land owned by the Church, and the Rev J T Cook, and Col. R P Davies went ahead with the transaction without checking with the Church Council. J Moy, one of the members of that Council was furious and was so incensed that he produced a Broadsheet which was handed to everyone within the Church. No copy seems to have survived, but it was to be sung to the 'Wearing of the Green' and the first verse was as follows:

'Oh neighbor dear,
Oh did ye hear,
The news that's going round.
Our Squire and Parson,
Want to sell,
Our bit of Parish Ground
It is a most distressful thing,
That ever yet was seen,
But some of the men in this town,
Are not so Jolly Green'

When the Tower was near completion, the Vicar, who seems to have been quite dictictorial and was not liked by many, had a dispute with Miss Barron, who had offered out of her own pocket to purchase a peal of Bells for the new Tower.

Firstly she was upset to see two of her Goats being given the 'order of the boot' by the Churchwarden, as they wandered into the churches cemetery. Not getting an apology, and with the Vicars high handed attitude regarding the selling of the Church land ensured Miss Barron did not give the Church anything, and within a short time, after some of her Goats had been placed into the animal Pound in Walton (opposite the Church) by people who knew they were hers, she decided she no longer liked Walton, and moved to Gt Holland.

Gt. Holland Church still has two original Bells. One dated about 1400

48

suggests that there had been a Tower earlier than 1413, and the other was made in 1460. These were increased to four in 1552 with a Sanctus Bell (possibly a handbell). In 1813 when a refurbishment was carried out, two of the 1552 bells were taken down and were not used. A Miss Muir in Walton bought these for £40. 1s 6d. and she gave them to Frinton Parish Church, but they were damaged when the Ivy pushed over the exterior Bell Tower, during the 1860's and two new bells were purchased from the Warner Foundry in the 1870's.

The two original Bells in Gt. Holland are still used during the last five minutes before Divine Service, and for Funerals. Miss Barron set up a Bequest, known as the 'Barron Bell Trust' to pay for Church Bells in various communities, and it was through her generosity that Kirby received two, to make a complete peal of eight.

It has always been believed that when she had the dispute with the Rector at Walton, she also at that time, changed the order she had made with regard to the set of Bells for Walton and arranged for their delivery directly to Gt. Holland Church, but this is quite incorrect, for the bells didn't arrive until over thirty years after Walton's Church Tower had been completed, and a few years after her death.

Walton has now only a single Bell. That which hung in the Old Church before 1798 disappeared and no church records have been established to show where the one they hung in the new Church came from, but it is possible that this was an earlier Bell, which was recaste by Thomas Mears, as it is dated 1804. It is known there was a Bell in 1297 and another purchased in 1458, but it is unknown whether it was either of these that remained, and which had been recaste. It is known that Robert Warner gave the Parish Church a Sanctus Bell in 1881, but there are no details as to whether it was a Handbell or a Hung Bell or what happened to it.

Not everything in the day to day running of the Church at Walton went smoothly. For centuries it was universally agreed throughout the country that 'waifs and strays' found dead on the beaches could be buried without ceremony of clergy, yet in 1867 the Vicar and churchwardens at Walton were fined £5 for burying a body, which had been washed up on the beach, in a box and not a coffin.

Kirby Church had a two dial clock installed in 1884, presented by Miss

Shum, and the clock at Walton was paid for by Col. Davies, who owned the Dairy farm. He gave a four dial clock, costing £160 which included the striking Bell, and made by J Smith and Sons of the Midland Steam Clock Works, Derby. In some books on the area, they state that it was Col. Davies who paid for the Tower, yet records show that the Church had a Tower fund, and basically Col. Davies was one of the largest contributors to it.

All of the Churches during the 1800's are known to have had organs, and in transition periods, both Kirby and Walton were known to have used for a brief period, a Barrel Organ that played Hymns. It could have been the same Barrel organ that was moved from one Church to the other, and it was known that one was kept in Thorpe during the 1800's, but as the years progressed the person turning the handle became arthritic and the hymns went as fast, or as slow, as his arms would allow. Eventually Walton gained a new Organ in 1882, with 790 pipes, made by Forester and Andrew of Hull who were the lowest Tender, at a cost of £304.

Kirby it is known had two organs in the 1200's and a single organ in the mid-1700's, although as within all Churches, they had utalised recorders and other early instruments. When they made the change to the more modern, they purchased a Seraphine in 1839, and actually employed a professional musician from Colchester to attend services and play it. Ten years later they changed to a Harmonium. In 1911, a new pipe organ was installed. At about this time, Gt. Holland were also to have a new 700 pipe organ.

In Frinton, they purchased a new Harmonium costing £10 in September 1863. Sixteen years later, another was bought, costing ten shillings more. Eventually a much finer and better American Organ was acquired in time to commemorate Queen Victoria's Jubilee in 1897, and Mrs Beadel who had been campaigning for a new Organ when her husband had been Vicar (1876/1887), was asked to play the new acquisition at the Jubilee commemoration service, as she had played the previous Organ on the first occasion it had been used during a service, eighteen years earlier.

Parish Churches were the heart of most towns, and the register of Baptisms, Marriages and Deaths often included relative comments to the times, such as in Walton in 1761 the words were added stating that 'there have been no deaths this year' whilst that in the 1764 register for Kirby

50

indicates that there were 'no burials this year, being the only instance this century' and, in 1759 when the local Tailor died, and after twenty years in the Town, they then discovered he was a woman. Gt. Holland's Register for 1629 states there had been 'no Baptisms that year.'

With change, other religions progressed in strength of calling. In all four towns the Methodists were to come and build. In Kirby Cross as early as 1820 there had been a 'Primitive' Methodist Church. Walton had a 100 seater Church in 1873 to take over from the one they had in Station Street (from 1849) and Frintons Methodist Church was built in 1896.

The Weslyns in the mid-1800's had a Church in Great Holland, and a new building was completed in 1928. From the 1840's they were known to have held services in Walton in private homes. They then used a room in Dorlings Hotel, and after this they used the Public Hall, but lack of members forced them to stop their gatherings in 1880.

The Quakers were in Walton from the 1820's, and were using as fellowship, members homes, with eventually Robert Warner purchasing some land by the Parish Church, and they built their Meeting House in 1878. It was to change, and became a Gospel Hall, then a Furniture Upholstry business, and it has now reverted back to being the Walton Gospel Hall again.

That 'very peculiar Army', the Salvation Army, were to hold their first meetings in Walton on the 9th July 1881. There were also open air meetings and, during August of that year, they also booked the Public Hall every night for gatherings. There was little reaction to their presence in Walton, but these were not the happiest times for the Army, and on one occasion in 1882, after 50 members from Colchester had attended an open air meeting in Walton, on their return to St. Botolphs they were set on by an unruly mob who threw eggs and missiles. The Army were to remain part of Walton life for over fifteen years but their growth in Clacton, especially after Gen. Booth purchased a home there, ensured the group in Walton eventually stopped regular gatherings, other than occasional Sunday meetings.

Spiritualism, Pentecostal, Christian Science, The Plymouth Brethren, all have or had places of worship. The Free Church in Frinton held it's first meetings in a house named Ingle Neuk in Harold Road in 1891 but with their growth, they eventually moved to their present site in 1896, a wooden building seating no more than 150 people. In 1912 the basic building designed by W Hayne was constructed and in 1935 the Tower and Porch were added. The Gospel Church in Frinton, and that in Walton were both to move from their original sites to settle where they are now.

The Catholic Religion came to Frinton and were using a Hut built behind the 'Queens Hall'. The 'Queens' had opened as 'Victors' initially, and was used for dances and Theatricals at a time when there was no other buildings of this nature within Frinton. As Kinomatograph programmes (silent cinema) grew in popularity, the name was changed from 'Victors', and when the Imperial Hall was built in the mid to late 1920's, the 'Queens Cinema' closed and the Catholics took it over. There was also a Catholic Church in Walton from the 1840's, but this was washed away, and another church was built in Saville Street. With the numbers attending and there being a Convent in Raglan Road Frinton, it was agreed that only one Church was required, and the one in Walton was closed. Congregationalists in Walton opened a Church in 1837, and moved it to Saville Street in 1853. A site in Station Street ensured growth and eventually the fine building seating 400 people was built in 1878. They have now become linked with the Methodists. The Baptists were in Hall Lane from 1925 and Plymouth Brethren in Saville Street in 1901. The Brethren were also in Old Road in Frinton for some years.

Many of the young religions have become part of the Towns. There are some that have a small following, and have not been mentioned and yet they are a central part of a few peoples lives.

Those discussed have been the important Religions within Britain, but there are others, which include the breakaway groups, emerging when people have become disenchanted. There have been a few Fundermentalist groups whose extreme attitudes have assisted in breaking up a few families. In addition a few cults have passed this way, and then there have been the Exclusive Brethern, The 7th day Adventists, Mormons and Moonies, as well as a few that have gathered in small groups and in private and there has been talk of Covens as Pentagrams have appeared at certain times of the year on the beaches.

52

Chapter 5   CHANGES FROM 1800

From 1800 the growth of Walton as a resort began, as the inland farming Village reached the Sea (or the Sea had reached it), every new building developed it's potential, and within thirty years it had 50 Cottages, shops and other buildings.

Edmund Aldridge had seen the potentials of Walton when he opened the Bath House Hotel in 1807. He had worked prior to this for the Nassau family of St. Osyth, who then owned much of the land within Walton, Kirby and Thorpe, and they had built the wooden structure which Aldridge was to buy, as their summer 'house'. He added a small number of rooms and created the Hotel. In 1810 a Gazetteer stated that Walton was a charming fishing village where 'at low tide you could see the Houses that had fallen into the Sea'. There was a road between the 'Bath House' and the edge of the beach, but for nearly eighty years, prior to a barrier being erected, when the Sea was rough, the water would overlap the road and flow into front of the Hotel, and Aldridge arranged that both the front and back doors be left open, so that the sea could pass directly through the building.

The 'gentry' began to make the journey to Walton. Officers in the Army, visiting the Martello Towers or checking the troops on guard (see chapter 13) seldom, unless they had to, would stop at the same place where the ordinary soldier slept, and so Aldridge, the ex-butler, had prospered. He did though have problems when it was discovered the Nassau family had built their house on land which they did not own.

A large tract of land had been purchased in 1739 by the Govenors of the Queens Anne Bounty, for the augmentation of the Rectory of Holy Trinity in Colchester, but it was too near Sea and most of the land had been washed away over the years, but the Summer House/Hotel was built on a small section that remained! It was some years after the Hotel had been opened that two laymen of Holy Trinity called to see Aldridge and inform him that he either pay them 'back' rent plus a fee for building on their land, or, he give them the Hotel. It was to cost him a lot of money. By 1848 the Hotel was advertised as having Hot and Cold Baths and that 'Hydropathic Treatments' were available.

Aldridge had the only Bathing Machine, which he then increased, as more were needed and by the 1870's he had sold out and Robert Swallow and J. Bates were eventually to become the largest owners of these Machines in Walton. A lesser number on East Beach were owned by William and Stephen Carter. The quantity of Machines had grown, because in 1841 a byelaw had been passed that 'no person shall enter the sea to bathe within one mile either side of the Jetty (The Pier) unless from a Bathing Machine'. Female attendants were on hand to assist the Ladies and the Children.

This Byelaw was changed after a year to specify that this restriction was to be only between the hours of 7 am in the morning and 9 pm at night as there had been complaints that no Bathing Machine was open outside of these hours. Some fifty years later this was to be altered again, when a Byelaw was created to stop people simply undressing on the beaches. Once this came into being, locals were having their own small Huts or tents where they could change and not have to hire a Bathing Machine each time they wished to swim. This in turn started the growth of the more permenant Beach Huts, and the eventual demise of the Bathing Machine. The era of Advertising was beginning when the sides of the Swallow and Bates machines had the words 'Beechams Pills' and other makers of Pills and Potions on them.

Bathing Machine owners also arranged the hire of Swimming Draws/Costumes and Towels. In 1879 there was a complaint that there were no 'Ladies Only' bathing machines. Bates wrote a letter to the papers stating he had two for this purpose, and a few years later a photograph was taken showing the machines, and the words 'Ladies Only' written on the sides of a number. There were also complaints in the press about the Swimming Costumes not being long enough, nor clean enough. Further letters from Bates appeared, stating they were quite long, 'for if they were any longer you would be able to step on the hem' and they were always washed after people had worn them.

The Machines were pushed as close to the Sea as possible as the tide went out, and then with the aid of a windlass and a long pole they would be brought back to new positions as the tide came in. Eventually each group had a strong horse for this purpose. Yet there were always problems regarding the Ladies of a delicate disposion. A letter from a lady in the newspaper stressed 'The Bathing Machines for men and women are

54

too close together'. When she left her Bathing Machine the tide was going out and the sea did not cover her ankles. The Costume was too short. 'All ladies machines must be some distance from men's, for both health and moral reasons'

From the 1820's the growth of Walton was evident. The Porto Bello Family Hotel was built, and was eventually to become a Commercial Hotel suited for Salesmen and Travellers. In 1825/6 'Navarino' a house on the corner of Saville Street, was built for William Lay and named after a battle from the Napoleonic War. These were all part of the beginning of modern Walton.

An appreciation of the poor standard of roads in those early days, gives an understanding why few ever visited Walton. (see Chapter 8). In 1830 it was indicated that 'Walton is hardly known, unless by inhabitants of Colchester to whom it has often proved a delightful summer residence'. After the Marine Hotel had been completed in that same year, there were then over a hundred rooms for visitors to Walton, in the Marine, Porto Bello, The Bath House and the various Boarding Houses, and within twenty years The Marine was advertising it had a hundred rooms, which was a 'sales gimmick', as there never were more than seventy rooms at any time when Dorling owned it. Land sold between North Street and Saville Street had within it's Deeds that 'No Butchers, Slaughterhouse, Blacksmiths nor Brick Kiln may be built, nor any business where a noisesome or offensive Trade should be carried out'. This land was known as Barnfield and included part of Saville Street. Walton at this time had only the one Miller, for John Archer had purchased both the Tide Mill and the Wind Mill. 'The Albion Hotel' was built where an apple Orchard had been in 1834, but the place was destroyed by fire in 1878, and the present 'Royal Albion' was rebuilt on the same site.

It really had only been the Copperas Industry and farming which had regularly brought outsiders to Walton before the 1800's, but from the 1830's people like John Warner, an owner of a Brass and Bell Foundry in London, visited what was a growing Town. He initially purchased five acres of land known as Sandfield in July 1834, and three months later a field known as Shopfield. It was in 1835 he started building East Terrace for himself, his wife and his fourteen children.

The Warner family were eventually to become the largest employer in the Walton area, with between 150 to 200 employees at an Iron Foundry, which was built in 1871/2. At the time Warner came to Walton, changes were already happening elsewhere. What was to happen in Kirby and Gt. Holland, and in Walton itself, also happened in many other parts of the Country, and labourers were to become available in Walton at the very time they were needed. Farm workers changed jobs to become builders and they became involved in the growth of the Town. They were required for the construction of the Railways. The growth in jobs at Warners Foundry, and then the builders moved on to create and build both Clacton and Frinton.

Up until this time most people living within the area had relied, either directly or indirectly, upon the earnings that Farming provided. In 1830, in Kirby, over half the population were employed in Agriculture and Farming generally. The others were the Shopkeepers, Inn Keepers and Beer sellers who all earnt from the wages of the Farming community. The remainder were the small number then working at the Quay in Kirby, many of whom again relied upon the results of farming, plus a few who were involved in Fishing, and of a total of nearly 900 people living in Kirby, the only people not working were the very young children, infirmed or to old to work. In the 1600's there had been a steady Woollen Cloth trade in Kirby, which mainly women produced at home, but the Industrial Age was to alter absolutely everything.

This was the time of Industrial revolution, and machines were being invented that would cut down the numbers needed to do specific jobs. At the end of the 18th century and into the 19th, farm produce prices were variable, and then they started to dramatically decrease. Grain prices went down radically, and accordingly, farmers could not afford to pay the same wages they had been paying their men (women and children), and whilst the monies originally had not been high, the lower wages ensured that starvation was becoming an end result in many families.

By the late 1820's large numbers of farm workers decided all over the country to go on strike. The problems were aggrivated when farmers decided they didn't need the previous number of hired hands, and had

56

started to purchase a 'new wonder of the age' - the Threshing Machine. This did the work of many, and in half the time. Suddenly workers realized their livelihoods were going completly. In December 1830 their anger reached a peak, and rumblings and rage developed into insurection and what was to became known in this area as the 'Tendring Hundred Riots' became a reality. This was not insular nor just a local event, but farm labourers were to run riot and be arrested for Rioting and destroying Threshing Machines throughout the length of Britain during this period.

Over a thousand men within the Tendring Hundred from Gt. Clacton, Bentley, Oakley, Beaumont and other places, were to gather in groups and set about destroying the machines in their areas. There were at least six Threshing Machines around Gt. Clacton and many hundreds of men gathered, marched and smashed to pieces every one of them.

At least 240 men from Kirby and Walton and over 100 from Great Holland, all went on the rampage. They victamised those that wouldn't join them. They stole tools from the Blacksmiths in Gt Holland and Kirby, and went to the farms of Samual Baker, Samual Wilson and William Scott. All had purchased these machines. Smashing them with hammers, the rioters naively believed that once the machines were gone, they would resume their normal, and previously good working relationship with their employers.

Once they were all destroyed, they returned to their local Inns and Ale Houses, happy with what they had acheived. Unbeknown to them, hundreds of Special Constables were being sworn in by the Magistrates at Thorpe whilst the troubles were happening, and they went to arrest the ringleaders. Two of the three that led those from Gt. Holland were seized that evening but the majority, by the time the Militia arrived, had already gone home. Many were to be hauled out of their beds in the middle of the night. The ringleaders were arrested from this area and they were held at Thorpe, until everyone involved, including those from Beaumont, Gt. Clacton, etc, were all captured. Then they were transported under armed guard to Chelmsford, where, over a number of days, these and many other similar cases from all over Essex were to be heard.

Of the 13 arrested one had actually worked 10 years on the same farm, another 16 years, but he was to die in Australia within six months of his arrival. Nine had originated from Kirby, one from Walton and three came from other areas. All were tried and sentenced within the week. Eleven received a uniform judgement of seven years. Two brothers from Kirby, James and Thomas Grant, both received 14 years. All of these were to be transported to Van Diemans Land (Tasmania in Australia). Charles Hicks stated one man from Gt. Holland received a life sentence, but he was mistaken. Had their actions happened ten years earlier, the law then would have produced hanging sentences for them all, but this was changed in the 1820's with death sentence only for Murder or Treason.

Within the month, the first batch of nine of the local prisoners were enroute in the prison ship 'Eliza', and two months later the remainder followed in the 'Proteus'. John Phipps from Kirby did not sail at this time, and his fate is unknown. It also has not been established whether any ever returned after they had served their time. Eight of the thirteen were married, most with children. Some wives and their families may have followed their husbands on this long journey, for the Government gave permission if they wished to go to Tasmania to join them. Two of the wives were to eventually remarry. One of the ringleaders from Gt. Holland had been earning more than most. He received 15 shillings a week, including beer, as opposed to an average wage of 11 shillings plus beer. All his efforts acheived was a free passage to Australia.

All of the 12 who travelled to Australia and lived throughout their term were to be given free pardons after only serving either five or six years, and this included the two who had 14 year sentences. John Ingram, was a real villain, having served time in prison before he was involved in the riots. Whilst in Australia he continually made trouble and was placed on diets of Bread and Water, put on Chain Gangs, and received on a number of occasions, 50 lashes. He was in fact immediately re-arrested after his pardon was given him. Most of the others were to serve their sentences quietly. There were a couple like Ingram who revolted against their treatment and received similar judgements which also included 10 days on the Treadmill or solitary confinement.

Not all the ringleaders from this area were caught. One man from Great Holland knew he would be arrested, and hid in Holland Hall Wood for many days before returning home. It was stated 'he became a changed man'. Once the Trials were over, no others were arrested. One farmer, whose machine was smashed, had his corn and some outbuildings destroyed by fire some weeks later. The arsonist (fire raiser) was never caught.

The Farmers were all recompensed in part by the Government for the machinery that had been broken up, and most re-bought Threshing Machines. The measures that had been taken ensured that the workers who returned to the same employers, never went on strike again. A few decided they wanted to get away from Britain, especially those that had not joined the strike and were still victamised by the others. The Poor Rates funded a few passages for complete families to go to Canada.

The overal changes created disenchantment, as large numbers had generations of ancestors that had been involved in farming, and they knew no other way of life. After the insurgence, a number of the employers, some of whom had also been in farming all their lives, sold up and moved away, with new people taking over, and most of these new owners having different ideas and attitudes.

A General Election at that time took place, which was a disgrace, whereby people who had the vote, were abused and threatened when trying to enter the polling booths and many were stopped from voting.

There was starvation. In Great Holland, a wagon load of bread was delivered for the poor. The person handling it, created difficulties, and the storehouse where it had been left, was looted, and everything shared out to those that were desperate. The four involved, who took away the bread, were all tried, but the Judge must have accepted their reasons as each only received six months 'hard labour' prison sentences.

This was the time of change. Walton needed workers to build houses, and to work in the brick works. Labourers who remained on the land were assisted with new agreements as a Union of Farmers was started to try and keep wages at an agreed level, then and in the future.

This was an age of Education. The rich would send their Children to Private Schools, either locally, or to the nearest Town, but of the rest of the population only a few could even sign their name. It was the wives of the clergy who were to assist and start many of the first schoolrooms.

In Kirby these lessons were taught only to the children of the workers, and initially classes were held in a hall beside the church, or within the Church itself. It was here that the overal term 'Sunday School' began, as these lessons were provided by the Vicars or the Curates wives throughout the Country on a Sunday morning, from nine to twelve, although in Kirby, because of the numbers involved, this was extended to two in the afternoon. The rest of the week, everyone worked.

In Kirby they started a series of Adult Education classes during the week but when the daylight hours grew longer, and the workers were able to continue working until late in the fields, the numbers attending the school diminished and eventually it closed through lack of support.

It was the Education Act of 1870 that changed things generally, and schools were to be open five and even six days a week from eight in the morning and stopping at two, enabling children to return home and assist their parents in whatever work they were employed. Children had to pay a penny a week for their Education, which was compulsary, as it assisted local Councils pay wages and the upkeep of the buildings being used, but, when money was short, some children simply did not turn up, especially when there were always parents that considered education a waste of time and money. At the age of 11 and then in later years, at 13, if it was shown 'they were learnt', they would leave, clutching a certificate indicating their knowledge (or lack of it). A school was built in Kirby in 1872 and in November 1899 it was condemed and the present building in Kirby Cross was quickly built in 1900.

In Walton the Vicars wife started a schoolroom at the Vicarage. This was only for the children of the towns labourers. There were by then two private schools and so a school for the growing Town was needed. Originally built in 1838, it had over 70 pupils by 1848. With the increase in population another building was built in 1853. By 1872 and the law stating every child must attend school, the numbers attending had outgrown the space and larger premises were built. This was enlarged twice, in both 1878 and 1886, and then, once again bigger premises were needed, which ensured the move to the school now in Standley Road. The 1872 School situated in the High Street, is now Walton Library.

60

A suggested way to effect growth in the late 1820's in Walton and attract more visitors, was to follow other Seaside resorts, and build a Pier, and at one oclock on July 2nd 1830 work began. It was stated it would cost £1000, but the public subscription did not raise enough, for the figure of £418 which the first part initially had cost, was still short of £47 three years after the first stage had been completed.

It had been designed by John Penrice, whose involvement with the Architecture of Walton during those early years was paramount. He produced designs for a Jetty (Pier) slightly longer than the 14 foot wide (four metre) by 150 foot long (48 metre) structure, with seating along the length. As money trickled in, the Pier was extended a further fifty foot, which had been part of Penrices original plan. In 1848 it was to be extended again, to 330 foot. Twenty years later another 70 foot was added, and in an attempt to gain competition from the 'new' Pier, which Bruff had built, a further 100 feet were added in 1871. An end length of 500 foot (about 150 Metres).

The very first commercial Boat to call at this Pier after it had been built in 1830, was the 10 ton Paddle Steamer 'The Joseph'. By 1833 the Ipswich Packet was calling three times a week with names like 'The Albion','The Father Thames' and 'The Metis'. Because of the length and the depth of the Sea, it was normal for people to be met by Rowing Boats either at the Pier, or by the Packet Boat, and to be rowed between the two. The cost of the journey at that time, from London to Walton, was either four or five shillings, which included the Boatman's fee. It was stated that anyone utalising any other Boatman would not have their monies refunded, and an additional 6d would be charged.

Pleasure boats were moored to the old Pier and ran trips to the Light ship. One was the 'Comet' owned by Mason and Cutter, and the other was the 'Secret' owned by Walter Smith, who was to become the Town Crier and was also the Piermaster of the first Pier in the 1870's. Both of these Boats were superceeded by the 'Bellissima' (The Bless your Heart) owned by Simey.

The growth of the Town was on. The Marine Hotel had been built by the creation of shares at £50 each. The first owner was Benjimin Kent who had R. Skitter as landlord. Over the years the names changed. Kent, Dorling and then Barker. It opened with 24 bedrooms and a small ballroom, but as the town grew, it eventually had 50 bedrooms, a 'Palace of Varieties', a Vinery and a Lawn Tennis Ground.

By 1830 when standing on the beach at Walton, there could be seen daily anything up to 300 boats, of which 200 would be Shrimp Boats and there were also many Sailing Barges. For years, Oysters that were eaten in Colchester and surrounds, originated in the Backwaters, but a combination of erosion and the growth of Boats into Landermere Wharf, ensured stocks diminished.One of the finest areas for Oysters was ruined by the stench and filth emerging after the sewers were built in the 1880's. Very few fishermen would go there because the smell was so bad, yet a small number, when times were hard, did obtain stocks from this obnoxious site, and it is presumed people were ill afterwards because of these tainted Oysters!

In April 1855 Peter Bruff had visited Walton and bought Burnt House Farm at an Auction held at the Porto Bello Hotel. The Farm was on the coast, halfway between Frinton and Walton. He also bought 100 acres of land that extended into what is now the centre of Walton. Realizing that the future of Walton was exceptional, he saw that a longer Pier, than that exisiting, was a major way (at the time) to bring people to the Town, and started building initally a Pier 300 foot in length. This then went to 600 foot by 1878. He was continually investing money in the Town, and by that time, owning land along the Coast near Great Clacton, which he had purchased in 1864.

He realized that the Pier was still far too short, based on the depth of the water at Walton, it needed a far greater length than even 600 foot to accomodate the larger 'newer' Paddle Steamers then being built. People were still having to be off loaded into rowing Boats when the Tide was out.

The old Pier was to collapse in November 1881 during a very bad storm, but Bruffs Pier was to attract more visitors the following year when it was lit by Gas lamp for the first time.

Bruff knew that to take the growing number of Boats, the Pier needed to be enlarged and lengthened again. To arrange this he amalgamated his Company with others (including the Steamship Line) to create enough funds to provide an extension to 1200 foot (about 380 Metres) and they also widened the Pier to take a Horse Tramway along it's length. It was after his death in 1900 that the Pier was sold and it was then once again developed, and this is often called the 'third Pier', although it was simply a massive extension to 2610 feet in length (about 850 Metres). When completed, the Electric Company installed Lighting along the length of the Pier in 1902, and the Tramway was also electrified. In the 1930's the tramway was changed to a small railway with a Steam Engine.

The Pier until the second world war was to be classified as the second longest in Britain (Southend being longer), but with the problems created between 1939 and 1945, and those since, the Pier is now the fourth longest in the country.

Bruff built the Clifton Assembly Rooms (also known as the Clifton Baths) in 1862 which were to contain many gentlemens pursuits, including billiards, a smoking room, etc. It even had an underground tunnel at the rear of the Hotel from the Round Gardens to enable gentlemen to visit the place without being seen walking through the front doors. Within two years Bruff realized the building was not financially viable, and it became the Clifton 'Hotel'. After the completion of the Pier, the Hotel was renamed, as it is today, as the 'Pier Hotel'. The Pier Hotel was the first building in Walton to have electric lighting. The Electric Company started in 1898

There were new houses, new shops and business's and Walton was growing.

> Walton how charming and for walking,
> And some distance it is not,
> I think in all the country.
> There could not be found,
>   a prettier spot.
>
> I can hesitate no longer,
> As to where to spend my summer days,
> For I must first go to Clacton,
> And then to Walton on the Naze

ANON

Chapter 6   TO NAME BUT A FEW

It would be foolish to point at three or four people and indicate that it was their drive and foresight which created the Walton and Frinton we have today. In over the last two hundred years there have been many changes and it's true a handful of names do crop up time and time again.

Edmund Aldridge building 'The Bath House Hotel' was possibly the first major move in creating a Seaside resort at Walton. The building was small and had dingy bedrooms. He did extend it at one point, but this was definitely the first Hotel. Aldridge also had the first Bathing Machine and the first Telescope which were both part of the selling factor of early Walton as a 'Seaside resort'

There would have been places to stay before the 'Bath House', for most medium sized villages had an Inn, and it is understood that Walton had at least two. The Falcon is believed to have stood on the site where the Porto Bello Hotel was to be built in 1825, and the 'Dukes Head' is also confirmed as having been within Walton as early as the 1500's. Both of these places would have had two or three beds available for Travellers, but other than the Angel Ale House, no other Pubs or Inns are known, and none of the names of the owners or landlords are known either.

From the year 1700, the village had been changing as it came closer to the Sea, with it eventually becoming a coastal Town. Within fifty years, by 1745, it had changed from being an inland Farming Community, into a Fishing Village and Aldridge was there from the 1800's.

He was to be followed by John Warner in the early 1830's. This happened when William Lay of Colchester had gone to look at Gt. Clacton at a time when there were very few houses on what was then the sea front, and little of the land was available to buy. Great Clacton was well in land and Clacton was not to start it's growth for another fifty years.

He was not impressed with what he saw, and decided to walk along the Coast, passing through Frinton and arrived in Walton. There he found a small and growing community and decided that he liked what he was seeing, bought some land and set about building a house for himself and his family. When talking to John Warner, a fellow Quaker, he expressed his pleasure regarding his new residence and it was natural that Warner would make a visit, as he was contemplating getting a property on the Coast. Warner also liked what he saw and began what became nearly a hundred years of Warner family linkage with the town. John Warner purchased two plots of land, and in 1835 started building East Terrace, a block containing seven Houses.

John Warner had opened Crescent Foundry in the 1790's at 8 Jewin Crescent, Cripplegate, within the area that is today the Barbican Library in London. They made initially Bells and some Brassware, but it was decided to enlarge the Brass side of the business, and the Bells were put on hold for fifty years.

London was changing, and Warner saw the need to get away to the Country whenever he wanted. He was wealthy. He had married his wife Esther on 20th October 1807 and they had three children. She though was murdered, and he was to marry her sister, as the law regarding such a marriage had just changed. They were then to have a further eleven Chilldren.

With a total of fourteeen children this was a very large family, which was to grow larger as they were to marry and they also had children. John Warner decided that the Sea and bathing were growing popular and he would obtain a property on the Coast to enable both he and his family to go to the Seaside whenever they wanted.

When in Walton, both he and his wife could stop at No.1 East Terrace, and if his wife decided to travel alone, then she could stay in her own property, Gothic Cottage which he built seperately for her. His family could select from the other six Terraced Houses if any of them came down. He built a cottage for his Coachman and properties for any of the staff not living in.

His enthusiasm diminished when he realized the distance to Walton ensured at least a days travel in both directions, and he also found that none of his family were interested after their initial visit. He then decided to get something more suitable in the countryside, and purchased a large property at Hoddesdon, and set about leasing off many of the places he had built in Walton, retaining only one or two for himself and his family. He died in 1852 and he had basically decided to pass the Foundry onto the first son of his second wife, C.Boreham Warner who was already working within the business. From that same marriage, was Robert Warner, who also was employed by the company, and amongst other things, it had been Roberts function to look after the properties in Walton. Then, on the 22nd July 1869 the elder brother died, and everything was automatically left to Boreham Warners sons, but they were not interested in working within a Foundry and Robert Warner took it all on.

So began a new era. Roberts consideration regarding Walton was apparent, when, prior to his becoming the owner of all the Warner holdings, he realized in 1864 that there would be a disaster as East Terrace was under threat from the Sea. It was the Walton Estate Manager, Samual Hibbs, whose Grandmother had been the Parish of Walton Overseer, that suggested a way to protect the Houses. Robert Warner gave Hibbs the go ahead, and over the following six months, in all weathers, Hibbs and three workers built the Promenade in the front of the Terrace, with additional breakwaters and the groynes which still exist today. This certainly did the job that was required. When Hibbs died in 1885, Robert Warner erected a tombstone to a 'Loyal and Faithful Servant'.

Hibbs efforts received Warners thanks, and in turn Robert Warner was made an Honorary Member of the Institute of Civil Engineers and eventually became their President, for all the work 'he' had done at Walton.

The outcome of his brothers death in 1869 was that Robert saw an opportunity to build a factory on the unused land they owned in Walton, and thereby enlarging the scope and various aspects of the London Foundry, which was soon to move to Spitalfields. By 1860 they had re-started making Church Bells again in London, and soon they were supplying Cathedrals throughout the world. Even the sound of quarter of an hour Bell within the Tower of Westminster is a Warner 'Crescent Foundry' Bell. The original Big Ben had also been a Warner Bell. The Walton Foundry produced new products, which included decorative Iron Seating for parks and municipal gardens. Portable Boilers for cooking 'in the field'. Also a range of large Pumps, mostly wind powered, and suitable for use in South America, in Plantations of the West Indies. On the Indian Railways, in Eygpt and other parts of the World.

66

Robert Warner had married Mary Ann Green. They had two sons and two daughters, and in the 1870's they were living in Chelmsford. It was in 1871 that he built the Walton 'Crescent' Foundry. This was completed within the latter part of 1872.

He was typical of many Quakers during this era. The Cadbury family at Bournville being a good example, whereby, as Cadbury had done, so too Warner started building houses for his workers and taking an interest in their welfare. Firstly Bloomfield Cottages in Hall Lane, then Canada Gardens in Saville Street and the terraced Houses on both sides of First Avenue. This area was to be called by the locals 'Foundry Village'. In addition, he built facilities for the workers including in June 1875 'Crescent Hall', which was designed by T A Cressy, and which become known as the 'Institute', where workers could eat their lunch, but, more important, it was also used for Adult Educational purposes in the evenings and the Walton Foundry Brass Band used it for their practice after their amalgamation in late 1875.

Alongside the Foundry he had dredged and built the Port Said Canal, where the heavy metal Pumps and Metal Windmills could be off loaded into barges, and these were then despatched to the Docks in London for shipment to various parts of the world. All orders were handled by the Brass and Bell Foundry in London, and their catalogue, showing what they produced, was a combined effort. At the foundry in Walton there was a Tramway to carry the very heavy goods within the premises, and when completed, to take them to the canal.

At one time, Robert Warner was to own White Lodge, Richmond Crescent and although a Quaker, he also owned the Albion Hotel which continued to sell Alcohol.

Some confusion happened after his death in 1896 when he willed everything to his grandson, Robert Marriage. His daughter Edith had married Andrew Marriage in 1879, and their son Robert had joined the Warner Company when he was old enough. The problem was that once the Grandson, who was then only aged 17, had the business, he first changed his name to Robert Warner Marriage, and then simply, to Robert Warner and started selling off everything the company owned. No.1. East Terrace became a small Hotel.

He did not have the same business foresight that either John or Robert Warner were known to have had, and there were business debts which he incurred (some suggest there were gambling debts as well) ensuring he needed money continually. The name Warner was from then on, no longer to be held with the same respect and reverence by the people of Walton, as inefficiency and incompetence at the top ensured people were laid off and eventually the Foundry was closed.

During the first World War it had produced Shell casings for 18 pounders and rigging for Aircraft. In Aug. 1945 the Foundry in Walton was sold to Harmers of Letchworth, who amongst other things produced Die Castings for Vauxhall and Pressed Steel, with some weighing over twenty tons. It also had a lucrative Piano Frames manufacturing base for many of the British Piano Companies. Harmers had to close eventually when outlets diminished. Now on the site is a series of varied business's utalising the ground area which once was Warners. The Canal is silted and the Tramway has gone.

In 1855 two things happened to add to the names of the people behind the building of Walton. In that year the Copperas works ceased producing Ink. They continued grinding, but the ink production passed to Harwich. In 1867 the works closed completly and J C Pawes purchased the site and built 60 houses, most of which are still standing.

It was also in 1855 that Peter Schuyler Bruff, an engineer originating from Portsmouth (born 1811/2) bought Burnt House Farm which had been owned by the vicar of Walton, Rev. Fenn. Bruff had been involved in the beginning of the Railways and other engineering ventures throughout the South and East of the country. He moved to Ipswich and reached the position as Engineer in Chief of the Railways for the Eastern Counties. He saw beyond Railways, and visiting Walton purchased the Farm and several parcels of land. At that time there were at least two fields between the Farmhouse and Barns and the edge of the Cliffs. When he was to sell Burnt House in 1879 and move to 'The Wick', in Frinton, one of the fields had gone and twenty years later the Farmhouse itself fell into the Sea.

Unlike Warner and Aldridge, Bruff knew ways of acheiving results, and started by getting the Walton Improvement Act of 1841 repealed to enable him to build the things he wanted. He resigned his job from the railways in

1857. Then visualising the potentials of Walton, he became the Godfather of the Town by creating Terraces, shops and buildings on his land. A Gas Works in 1862. A Water Works was needed for only some houses had their own wells and water was having to be brought from Kirby daily. Bruff sunk a deep artisian well and had the water steam pumped into a large tank, which was big enough for the whole town.

Robert Warner also sunk a well of over 360 foot (120 metres), in an attempt to assist the Town, and create some form of competition, for Bruff's Water charges were acknowledged as being excessive. Possibly Warner felt that by using the large Windmills the Foundry were manufacturing and which were being used in pumping in other parts of the world, he could create an advertisment for their use within Britain, by providing a cheaper way of obtaining the water from depth, as oppossed to the Steam driven system Bruff was using.

Until Bruff arranged a direct piped route from Mistley's Water Works, the water produced from his well was brackish, made foul tasting tea, and was like water from other 'watering holes' elsewhere, whereby it served as an alternative and a Tonic. It was though far better than the little amount that Warner managed to get pumped up, and, in the end, Warner had to take the people boreing the hole to court for the lack of 'water' which they had promised and it is presumed for the lack of sales he had hoped to create for his Windmills.

A Warner Metal Windwill was built and used locally. This stood for a number of years by the Cricket Ground in Frinton, and was used to draw up water which was used for irrigation purposes. A pond by the grounds is still known as 'Windmill Pond'.

Until a pipeline from Mistley was constructed, as indicated, the charges for water were very high. The Clifton Hotel was, during the season, spending nine shillings a day in purchasing what they needed from Bruffs Water Works. In 1990 prices, at least fifty to sixty pounds a day

The Paddle Steamer lines, which had attempted to call regularly at the old Pier, transfered their alligence to Bruffs. He probably had shares in the Company, but it was mainly through his personal contacts that he developed and offered the shipping owners increasing facilities at the new Pier.

Like many entrepreneurs, he was always looking elsewhere, and he had purchased a large plot of land on the Sea edge near Great Clacton, but it wasn't for a few years that he began to develop modern Clacton. Amongst the first things he built there was a Pier, and in so doing ensured that the Paddle Steamers would call at both of his Piers in Walton and at Clacton.

It must be understood that whilst he instigated these moves, he was only partially involved financially, as he set up business's which involved shares, investors, and under various company names including that of 'The Marine and General' or the 'Walton Pier and Hotel Company'.

At one point he became split in three, with regard to work needed at Walton; looking towards what he would do in Clacton; and then, during this same period, his involvement as the Engineer Director of the Tendring Hundred Railway bringing the line that was to eventually reach Walton. This ensured his Pier and his Railways were to become the two important sources of income for the Companies he was involved with.

He had looked at Frinton, and tried to buy both the Glebe Lands from Richard Stone, and also the Farm lands owned by Hicks. Maybe it was their rejection that made him purchase the plot of land that was to become known, and grow into Clacton.

Hicks had built 'The Wick' in 1860, but it wasn't until after his death that the House and lands were to be purchased by Bruff. Based on his potential plans, after buying and moving into 'The Wick' he put forward a scheme for a Tramway between Walton and Frinton. This was rightly rejected by the Walton Council, for at that time there were only a handful of people living in Frinton.

Predominently Bruffs main plan for Frinton was to create a new Town, which he decided to name 'Frinton Haven'. After buying the land in Clacton and then in Frinton, plus his work in Walton, ensured he started having financial problems, and he had to bring in more people to create enough monies needed to extend the Walton Pier (again).

His influence was such, that the elders of Walton asked him to remove the original, and by then, derelict Pier in June 1882, because they stated that Visitors were leaving the town early because the wreckage of old pier was

70

'an eyesore', and during October 1882 he employed a team of men to take it down.

By 1889 he had changed his mind regarding Frinton and sold off his holdings to Richard Powell Cooper. Bruff had been continually purchasing properties within Walton into the 1880's, but then he set about selling everything to concentrate all the finances and effort within the new town of Clacton. By doing this, his links with Walton and Frinton were to be slowley broken, other than the erection of two Stained Glass windows. One to his mother in Frinton Church, and the other to his memory in Walton Church which was placed in position in 1901 after his death in 1900.

It has often been suggested that it was the Richard Stone family that started modern Frinton. What is forgotten is that there were a total of four generations of Richard Stones, and none of them did anything for the area, other than rebuilding the small Church and farming the Glebe lands. In 1883 Richard Stone III sold everything to Richard Powell Cooper of Ipswich. Bruff had attempted to buy these lands, but he had been turned down continually as the family saw what he was doing to Walton. Cooper offered a degree of gentility.

Powell Cooper in 1888 purchased from Bruff all the land he owned in Frinton and it was here that Cooper set about creating the town which exists today. In fact he continued to utalise some of the ideas that Bruff had put forward regarding 'Frinton Haven' to ensure it became something more than just 'another' new town.

What Powell Cooper stated in the newspapers at that time, was that, within Frinton, there would be No Public Houses, No Boarding Houses, No Public Transport. No Rubbish would be allowed to be burnt until after 5 pm (1700 Hrs) on a Sunday, and the Greensward would be free of Picnickers and Visitors. The rubbish burning and the Picnickers on the Greensward were always considered to have been Bye-laws after this statement of intent and made just over a hundred years ago, but they were never instigated. For many years residents have been known to approach and stop visitors picnicking, by suggesting that they were 'breaking a Bye-Law' when none actually existed. There was for a period signs put up which 'requested' people not to picnic, but again, this was nothing more than a way of keeping the mythology that had been mentioned a hundred

71

years earlier, alive and well.

Cooper ensured that each house being built would be of a high standard. Detached and in it's own garden, and with no front fences. Anyone buying a plot of land within Frinton had to agree to build an expensive house costing not less than £500 in 1889, (about £200,000 in 1990) but not build any place where Alcohol could be sold. Also, that you agreed, and it is still in most peoples Deeds, not to have a caravan parked on your land.

Bruffs original plans for Frinton had included a Market, a Tidal Basin and it becoming a Marine Resort. These were all scrapped, including a Jetty (Pier) which was started in 1887 but was stopped when Bruff sold out. It was being built in line with the end of Connaught Avenue.

Frinton had arrived.

There are three other names that are valuable in memory.

In Walton in 1881, Phillip Brannon set about building a new Town at the Naze, alongside that exisiting. So began the Naze Park Estate which was on land that Brannon had purchased. He believed that an 'up market' select section, within the Town of Walton, was needed.

He visualised a Hospital, a Pier which would have been bigger and better than Bruffs, Sea Defences, Tearooms. Amongst other things a large house was constructed, known as the Mabel Greville, which became known as 'Brannons Folly'. It was for some years to become the 'St Osyths Home of Rest by the Working Girls Protection Society of London'. There is the possibility that the Foundry and Foundry Village were too close to the project and this could have been a major contributary factor why these plans were never fullfilled. Brannon appears to have been a dreamer, who had vision, (see pages 90 and 134) but never enough monies to take anything he started much further than the planning stages.

There were other names and other schemes. In 1961 Godfrey Evans, a well known English Cricketer, proposed to build a 78 acre Estate on the Naze with 350 houses, bungalows and Flats, swimming pool and an 80 Bedroom Hotel but this was wisely (in retrospect and based on the present

72

state of the Naze) rejected, but the name that does stand out, is that of the Frinton Park Estates, yet remembered not for what they acheived, but for what they didn't complete (see following chapter)

CHAPTER 7 TIMES OF THE GREATEST CHANGE

Specific dates and the small number of known individuals who created the changes within the area are one thing, but, at the end of the day, life for the four villages (Towns) as they became interwoven, need to be understood. Kirby and Great Holland remained fairly static for over a century, whilst Walton and Frinton grew. In 1880 a 15 year old domestic was earning only two shillings and six pence a week (or £6. 5O pence per year) all found, and a woman working on the farms was fortunate to earn six pence a day (Two and a half pence in todays money). These like so many others are the forgotten people, and yet they were, and remained, the backbone of the community..

Great Holland from 18OO was written about by Charles Hicks, a local Farmer, within his diary, which make interesting, although at times, insular reading.

At the turn of the 19th Century, there were a few cottages in Great Holland and more were being built. Labourers were generally 'uneducated, ignorant and a rather outlawed race of men' In the middle of the village was a water pump and whilst it was used by the majoiry, many of the larger houses had their own wells In 1806, a serious fire swept through the Mill House, although the windmill was saved. This was a time when a growing number of workers at Great Holland Hall and at the farm, started to ride to work on donkey's (many of whom came from Kirby), and it was their employer who had to feed and keep these animals during the day. This annoyance was aggrivated by the incessant braying throughout the day created by the number that were gathered. There were over 26 at one point, and the local gentry, even those without staff who had donkeys, based on the complaints, devised a method of getting rid of the them by stating that as the rates were due to rise, that anyone with a Donkey would not be suitable for Poor Relief. This ensured everyone was soon to be walking to work again.

The poor rate (relief) was based on anyone living in a community, who were classified as destitute, could apply for monies to keep them and their family in enough food for a period of up to one week. One man in Gt. Holland continually applied, although he had a good job, but once he obtained his wages, en-route home, he would always call in on 'The Ship' in Gt. Holland. He would then remain there, often joined by his wife, and sometimes for up to three days at a time, until they had spent every penny of his earnings. Every Monday or Tuesday he applied at the magistrates for money. Always he was reprimanded but he was still given enough so he, and his family, could live until the following payday.

In 1832 times were so serious throughout the Country that there were fifty five people claiming Poor Relief in just Gt. Holland, which represented about an eighth of the population, and this was costing a total to the Parish of £10 each week (at least £5000 in 1990's money).

In Kirby there had been a workhouse built in 1815, but this was closed in 1840, and the building was altered and it became six cottages with a bakehouse in the centre. The inmates (who were few) were then sent to Workhouse in Tendring. Eventually the Bakehouse was removed and two cottages were erected in it's place.

The Lawyer, the Doctor and the Dentist seldom came to Kirby, Gt. Holland or Frinton, and everyone had to go on specific days to Walton, or if urgent, to Thorpe, to see any one of these. All three were expensive, and most people only called on them as a last resort.

From the earliest days, those that knew about Herbs were normally the first to be called on by the poor (whilst the gentry would call out the Doctor). In the early 1800's a man named Reed, a Herbalist living in Walton was summoned to Great Holland to visit James Francis a carpenter who was very sick. Reed knew immediately what was wrong and made up a concoction which he then started ladeling down the mans throat. The Man vomitted everything he had been given. The 'Doctor' repeated the dosage, and the man was sick again. This was continued. The mixture repeatedly being pushed into his mouth, and man being ill each time, and getting weaker and weaker. In those days small amounts of poison were often considered a good form of medicine, but it is unknown whether this was

74

part of this medication, except that eventually the man died still being made to take the remedy. At the Inquest it was stated that Reed was lucky not to have been charged with murder, and with the finger being pointed at him, he left Walton within hours of the findings being completed. Two hundred years earlier he would have been classified as a witch and hung.

The lack of monies ensured that amenities we all take for granted today, simply did not happen. The instalation of Street Lighting in Kirby only took place in 1930. Tapped water had become available for the first time forty years earlier with a single outlet in the middle of Kirby Le Soken. It came from a spring on Col. Blanchards Farm and as the need was apparent, he eventually arranged seven taps in various places, and these remained available until water was piped from Mistley to Kirby, and only then, during the mid-1930's, were homes to eventually have running water.

In Kirby when innoculations first began, mothers were encouraged to bring their children to Kirby Post Office on certain days, where, as an incentive, once over, the ladies were handed a penny, so they could get a pint of Porter from the Royal Oak Ale House next door.

In 1887 over 110 children attended the Sunday School Treat in Kirby where normally entertainment was generally of a local nature. A Brass Band made up of players from Kirby and Gt. Holland met regularly from the 1890's. They accompanied at open air religious 'Camp Meetings' and they played at local Fetes and Fairs. During these, and earlier times there were no holidays as we know today. Originally only Christmas Day, Boxing Day, and Good Friday were all that workers had off. Bank Holidays didn't begin until 1871. There were no annual holidays. Everyone worked six days a week. Only Sunday was free. Many employers did allow their staff time off to visit the yearly 'Fair' but generally on the understanding that they would work extra hours to cover the time off they had spent 'enjoying' themselves.

At the turn of the century, the local Barber cut hair at 2d, shaved for a 1d, and cut your corns for nothing. Fresh Milk was a penny halfpenny a pint, but after twelve hours this dropped to a penny a pint. Skimmed milk was a halfpenny a pint but three pints could be had for a 1d after twelve hours.

Parish or Council Houses were being built throughout the 1800's and 1900's, and yet, because they were what they were, their standards were

75

never high, and in 1930 some of the Kirby Council Houses were classified as being 'filthy' even before anyone went to live in them.

Even in the 1930's it was still a Tradition in this part of Essex to throw into the empty house Bread and some Coal when it had been completed and it was ready for people to live in, to ensure that those who took it over would always have enough food and heat

When the Walton Improvement Act was produced in 1841, it was done in an effort, through the rates, to improve the Town, whereas in fact it did little and parts were never to be implimented. A section of that act stated that the Streets should be cleaned daily by people employed for the purpose, and they would water the roads as well in an effort to keep the dust down during the summer months.

By 9 am each morning it was requested that every Resident should sweep (or make arrangements to have swept), the front of their homes. By 1882 the main streets were still being watered and cleaned, but the side streets were ignored and were generally filthy and filled with rubbish.

It was also decided in 1841 that no houses would be allowed to be built with a Thatched roof, because of the problems created if there was a fire.

It was suggested within the Improvement Act that everyone within Walton should contribute towards a Sea Defences System. The Council then changed it's mind and decided that 'anyone having a house near the sea must pay for their own Defences'. This is an argument, as to the needs, and who pays, which have continued for nearly one hundred and fifty years. It was the bigger property owners who found they were being asked to cover all of these expenses, although the whole town gained from the work that was being done. Bruff and Dorling always seemed to be arguing about this. It has been suggested that this continual haressment in getting Bruff to pay for a lot of the work, ensured that Bruff in the end decided to invest completly in Clacton, which, until his death in 1900, he was to virtually own, leaving Walton, as he did, to it's own devices by the late 1880's.

In 1563 John Sadler had given 35 acres to Walton which produced enough money in annual rent to cover the needs of the poor. Over the years, with extensive erosion, the land continually decreased in size, and accordingly the Town Rates were increased to cover both the communities needs and the requirements of the poor. It was the richer locals, like Miss

76

Barron who ran the private school 'Erith', or the Churches that tried to assist the poor, especially at Christmas. Miss Barron was a philanthropic individual who was treated with a degree of scorn and laughter by residents. She was looked upon as an eccentric because of her love of Goats, which actually lived in the house with her (the school being elsewhere), yet she was kind hearted and always gave to the poor blankets as well as wooden sleepers for their fires. Even when she moved away from Walton she continued this generosity by providing Coal or Blankets at Christmas for the poor of Great Holland.

In Kirby, Frinton and Gt. Holland, the Churches used monies gathered from renting their Glebe lands to supply the poor with goods at Christmas. In Frinton Richard Stone listed the gifts of money or goods he handed out. Those with money like Col. Blanchard or Ambrose Law in Kirby and Walton passed out Christmas gifts of either blankets or Coal.

In Walton in the 1890's there was a degree of local entertainment. There were two Brass Bands: Warners Foundry and the Town Band. It also had a Choral Society. Amateur dramatics. A String Orchestra. On Albion Beach and at East Terrace for the visitors were two Camera Obscura, the Victorian 'modern wonder'. There had been for a number of years, in the 1860's, a Drum and Fife Band, who wore special Tunics and Slouched hats.

A Childrens Museum was opened in July 1881, in Station Road, owned by Mr Florey, that comprised solely of a few stuffed birds; some Models of Churches and Buildings that he had made, and a large Music Box. Mr William March the dentist would set up surgery every other Tuesday, as he lived and worked in Thorpe. A Bank was to open in Walton, the 'Mills, Barrington and Bawtree's Bank'. North Street in the 1880's was lived in by Tradesmen or Mechanics. Both were classified in those early days, as being quite inferior persons.

The main complaint was that even in 1882 there were few footpaths alongside roads anywhere within Walton. The main throughfares were to await until the late 1880's before pathways and kerbs were to be laid as carts, carriages, horses, and eventually the Motor Car, became more numerous and therefore dangerous to pedestrians.

Many larger Cities had Town Criers. Walton felt they should not be alone, and from the 1850's they had an irregular who walked the Town.

77

Amos Grant was to be the Cryer from 1888. James Smith, a year or two earlier always started and finished by shouting 'God Save the Queen and her Loyal Subjects'.

Four photographers lived at one time or another in Walton before 1910. T. Dunningham arrived in the 1850's and he was followed by J. Jones; T.C. Brooks and A. Azulay over the next thirty years. There was a Circulating Library and a Reading Room, yet Kirby were not to have a lending Library until 1931.

On the second Tuesday in October, every year, all Traders shut their shops in Walton, and took an annual one day family holiday together. Trips to Felixstowe by the Boats, or in later years, by Charabanc (the open topped holiday buses) to various parts of Norfolk or Suffolk. This 'day off' continued after early closing was introduced in Walton in 1881, and up until the 2nd World War. Nobody opened on a Sunday.

In Walton for Queen Victoria's Jubilee in 1897, a Clock Tower with a water fountain, designed in 1894, was suggested but insufficient monies were gathered, and just a Drinking Fountain was built instead. Forty years later this was replaced as a gift by the Walton Visitors Association.

In Frinton they proposed a Drinking Fountain for the Jubilee, but could only afford a Garden which cost £200. For Edwards Coronation, in 1902, a fine Clock Tower was proposed, but only enough for a Drinking Fountain was gathered, and ensured they built the one that had been designed for the Jubilee five years earlier!

In 1897, after the building of the Electric Power Station in Walton, the lights in the streets were to be changed slowley from Gas lamp to Electric Light. During this transformation, Ernest Luff, the man who was to start 'Luffs Bible Bookshop' in Frinton, was employed to cycle around Walton and Frinton as the Gas Lamplighter. There were thirty Gas Lamps in the streets of Frinton at that time, and in Walton there were very many complaints that the street lighting was in certain parts of the Town, not enough.

For many years after the Napoleonic wars the Military regularly camped on the Naze, and amongst the various Regiments that came were the Hon. Artillary Company who stayed a few times in the mid-1800's. In later years, the Military were to be followed by other groups, including the

78

New Zealand Champion H.A.Parker winning the first Frinton Tennis Tournament in1902. Note the Club House, which was given to Kirby in 1927.

A print from the sales brochure that was produced to sell shares for the Marine Hotel. The booklet looks like a guide, and was produced in 1829, but examination, both of the guide itself and the picture, shows that the building had not been built at the time it was produced. The Hotel was built in 1830

The original Pier as seen by the son of John Constable, Alfred Constable c1832

'East Essex Ironworks' Great Holland. On the left is founder Henry Ratcliffe with his daughter Grace standing holding a Ratcliffe Bicycle, and in the cart, son Archie with their pet dog   c1908

Mr and Mrs Frank Turner in the doorway of their sweetshop, and in the other doorway, a young Ernest Luff when the Bible Bookshop was in Old Road. Whilst the Turners are now forgotten, the man who took the shop over will always be remembered, because Mr. Huckle had two thumbs on his left hand   c 1904

Frinton Post Mistress Mrs Smith, stands at the right side of the picture and beside her son Albert, and her daughter, Mrs Clouting. In front of them is little Charlie Clouting. Amongst the Postmen and boys is Senior Postman Horace Sparling (3rd Left) and Lifeboatman Billy Hall (6th right)

The Windmill at Great Holland
  c1912

The Albion Beach with Bathing Machines and a Camera Obscura in the foreground   c1894

V.A.C. (Voluntary Auxillary Company) and the Y.M.C.A. These later camps as such were the fore-runner to the Holiday Camps of the 1930's and Post War years. The Willow, Jubilee, Coronation Camps and the Martello Towers.

The Boats that came to Walton altered as the style of Piers changed. Initially it was the 'Queens' with the 'Queen of Orwell' calling on alternate days at the 'old' Pier, but the companies alligence then moved to the 'New' pier.

The small group of Paddle steamers became the Woolwich Steamboat Packet Company and then they changed their name to the London Steamboat Company as they amalgamated with others throughout Britain. One of the next generation of Boats to make the journey to Walton were the 'Belles'. The 'Walton Belle' was one of seven and was built in 1897, which ran from Felixstowe to Walton, and then, changing boats, your journey could be continued to London by taking the 'London Belle' that ran from Walton to London. None ran direct from London to Felixstowe at this time. The Company changed it's name again to become the General Steam Navigation Company and the era of the 'Eagle' Steamers began, and they continued calling at Walton throughout the 1930's.

Eventually the 'Royals' emerged, with 'The Daffodil' making just one or two journeys in early 1948, travelling from London to Walton. There was just a half hour tie up, but, because of the depth of these boats, based on the shortened length of the Pier after the War years, they were considered too dangerous when the Tide was low, as their propellors stirred up the mud so much that the end of the Pier became unsafe and this was the demise of an era, as Railways and Buses had already taken over the transportation of the crowds to Walton. Clacton Pier continued to receive the Boats for trips to France or to Margate long into the 1960's.

In the 1920's after the first World War, people started to come to Walton regularly from the East End of London, and by word of mouth, the numbers grew, and eventually they had their own August Visitors Association. Yearly each family were informed of the events being offered, including Football and Cricket matches against Walton Teams, Sandcastle Competitions, and a Childrens Sports that often had over 600 entries.

They hired the same Beach huts every year, and stayed at the same Hotels and Boarding Houses. The two weeks altered, but the growth in numbers continued up until the Second World War. After it was over, they started again, but life and attitudes were changing, and whilst many couples were to have met during their pre-war two weeks stay, and some eventually were to get married, the sun of Spain and cheap holidays overseas ensured that Walton's popularity was to diminish and the August Visitors Association came to an end.

It was in Walton in 1934 that the 'Bath House Hotel' was pulled down, and another built on the same site. Visitors had for years misnamed the original as the 'Beach House Hotel' for the road between it and the sea was generally covered throughout the year by sand. Donkeys were then tethered officially at specific points for rides, although at one time in the 1870's, Donkey owners had them spread all over the Streets and the beaches, and a Bye-law had to be introduced to stop this practice, especially when in 1881 J Osborne was fined for allowing seven Donkeys to race through the streets of Walton 'to the endagement of life and limb of the people on the streets' at a time when there were no Pavements, and special licences were issued from then on to the Donkey attendants/owners.

Frintons growth was a late starter, with restrictions placed on new residents by Powell Cooper. Prior to taking over the Estate, there were a number of aspects of Frinton long forgotten. There had only been one main Road going to the Sea from the Gates, which is now part of Connaught Avenue that then led into, and along 'Old Road' with Pole Barn Lane going Eastwards, and Witton Wood Road went West.

There was a path that passed alongside St. Mary's Church and went across the Marshes to Great Holland. At that time there was only a small number of buildings which represented Frinton. The Church and standing by it The Hall. There had, over the centuries, been a number of Frinton Hall's and as each fell to the Sea, another was built.

In 1760, on the site of an earlier Farmhouse and it's Barns, 'The Wick' was built, and which is now Frinton Library. There was the 'Parsonage', but the truth of it's origins are now masked in time. The Cottage stood on Parson's Field, and it was stated that this was owned by a man named Parsons, and which, eventually the Parson (the Vicar of Frinton) was to use, by the 1870's, and it then became known as the Pasonage. There had

80

been a Farmhouse, out houses and Barns and two or three cottages prior to the building of 'The Wick'.

In Pole Barn Lane, there was still, even as late as 1898 at the Sea end, a very large Barn called appropriately, Pole Barn. When the Martello Tower was built on the Greensward, two cottages were placed alongside it. One was for many years to be lived in by John Popperwell, who was Richard Stone's coachman, the owner of Frinton Hall, and the other was lived in by a Coastguard, until both cottages eventually collapsed through subsidence.

There was a problem regarding Postal matters until a Post Office was opened at the bottom of Connaught Avenue. All Post for Frinton was delivered to Kirby Post Office, but anyone wanting a Money Order had to go to Walton. Mail was delivered to Frinton from Kirby the 1890's by Horace Sparling, who was the son of the Kirby Postmaster. He would walk and then eventually he used a pony and trap for this purpose. When Frinton had it's own Post Office, Sparling became the Senior Delivery Man.

In 1886, Frinton was classfied as 'the most old fashioned of Essex Villages' although at that time it was still basically a hamlet, and nothing more.

By 1889 over fifty houses had been built in Frinton, yet in 1891 only a small number had been sold and the town had increased by only thirty people. Powell Cooper realized that something was needed to draw people to 'his' town and why in 1895 he decided to lease a large tract of the marshland and a year later created the Golf Club.

The earliest problem with Frinton had been water. There were four ponds of varying sizes in Frinton but no wells, and it needed nine miles of piping to bring water from Mistley. To ensure a continual supply in all weathers, as the original piping was known to fracture on occasions, a Water Tower was built in 1902, and was continually filled with pumped water. This remained in position for ninety years. Prior to the water pipes being installed, for the first few years of the town, water had been brought by cart from Kirby, and was sold at a half penny a bucketful. This was just one of the reasons why people would not buy properties in Frinton initially.

Another reason for the lack of house sales, during those formative years was the mud, as no road was laid until two thirds of all the plots of land in any street had been sold. For years, mud was the order of the day, ankle deep during rainstorms, and a setback in trying to sell the properties.

R T Weatherall of London, designed much of the Town as it is now. His plans were devised in 1883 for Bruff, and these were continued after Powell had purchased 'Marine and Generals' holding. Weatherall was to be employed as the Districts surveyor for many years. One of the earliest arrangements was a drainage scheme for the Town in 1899, which still exists. Originally the Towns lighting system was Oil Lamp. Gas was then piped from Walton and eventually Electricity was to be produced by the Frinton Light Company which was based in Pole Barn Lane.

Most of the earliest Frinton properties were designed by either A. Douglas Robinson or R J Page, although one house 'Homestead' in Holland Road, had major architect Charles Voysey involved, and when built, it was to be described as a Modern Middle Class Villa. It was next door to this house that Mrs Wallace Simpson had her residence, and which Edward, The Prince of Wales, was known to visit.

During these years it was proposed that Walton and Frinton should be amalgamated as one Town, and in 1886, it had even been put forward by Bruff that Walton should become a suburb of Frinton, yet in the end, they were both to become linked together as part of an Urban District Council in 1896. In 1934 they were joined by Kirby and Gt. Holland.

It had been decided by Bruff that the centre of Frinton was going to be at a point in Ashlyns Road, where Upper Fourth and Fourth Avenue at present meet. Fourth Avenue was therefore the first road to be developed, going towards the sea.

All building plans were based on the original Estate Manor borders. When the Railway was built, it did not enter Frinton at all, for until the 1900's, the houses backing onto the Railway along Pole Barn Lane were still in Walton, whilst, on the other side of that same road, the houses were in Frinton. In 1905 15 acres were passed from Walton to Frinton, and a number of anomolies were then corrected. The present Frinton Community Centre at the Triangle, as well as Tendering High School, are both in Walton. People from Great Holland and Kirby have to add the wordage Frinton on Sea to their mail, otherwise it gets sent to Clacton for sorting, and can lose up to a day in delivery time. A hundred years ago, all mail being sent to this area had to have the wordage Colchester added to it for

82

basically the same reason.

One thing that did not immediately change after Walton had passed the 15 acres to Frinton, was the Ecclesiatical borders, whereby those nearest the Railway line were still within the Parish of Walton. If anyone living there wished to marry, they had to have their Banns read in Walton Church, and at one time, actually marry there as well, even if they were regulars at Frinton. It took a further Eighty years before the Diocise acknowledged that they were a step behind everyone else regarding what was in Frinton and what wasn't, and they were to change their borders only in the late 1980's.

The main changes visually in Frinton took place only after tons of earth created a massive landslide along the front in 1901. Powell Cooper who owned the land, gave the frontage to the community (realizing he would have to pay for what was going to be needed if he did not) and the outcome was the Frinton Sea Defences and Improvement Act of 1903. Initially £20,620 was spent on Sea Defences and the cliffs. Then a further £12,000 was spent on the Greensward (which means a turfed area of land) and landscaping.

Freutuna looks on the Greensward
And the Greensward looks of the Sea,
Resting there three dreamy hours,
I then rested yet another three.
ANON

The grassed area exisiting prior to the Greensward, had been used for years for playing Football and Cricket matches, and the Greensward continued to be used for many Sports and Public Events. The Church Fete for St. Marys started after the Greensward had been laid, and this actually developed into the Horticultural Show which still takes place today, although it is no longer held on the Greensward. One of the varied prizes at these early Flower Shows was for the finest piece of Copperas on display.

Hotels started springing up in Frinton. The Queens, a Hotel now gone, in the earliest days offered fine entertainments and for years had alongside it a Bowls Green. It was built in 1888. The Grand, was designed and owned by F F Ramuz with 50 bedrooms and had been built in 1898 by R J Moore.

The Rock was built in 1895 and the Maplin in 1911. There was also the Esplanade, The White House and especially the Beach Hotel, whose dances were classified as 'exceptional'.

Frinton was growing, yet residents in 1902 were shocked to see a 120 foot aerial erected alongside a house in Upper Third Avenue. Marconi's of Chelmsford had purchased a house, No.24, and started the first Wireless Telegraphy School in the world. They also purchased the house next door, and a dozen ex-graduates became students for three years where they all lived and worked. There was a sub-station in Pole Barn Lane, and with Marconi's need for Electricity they invested a large amount of money into the new Electric Works that was to be built there. With the power they acheived, they managed to link with Chelmsford and Harwich, and it was attempted to get the first messages over water, across to Southend. The aerial was then raised a further Forty Five feet at one point.

This school was unusual, especially in early 1901, whereby the students were all paid to study there. The Managing Director decided that as they were students he need not pay them, and it was known that he was considering that future intakes of students would be on a different understanding. Whether things changed or not is now unknown excepting that many of those first group of 12 were to rise to become Directors and managers of the firm in later years.

Locals asked what the tall stick was (the aerial) and they were told quite seriously (tongue in cheek) that it was being used for a new type of semiphore, based on it's height. It was seen to have a lot of movement and many believed this. Others who asked, were told that the mast had been erected by the Sea so they could send messages along the tops of the waves, and it is here the term 'Wavelengths' and 'Wavebands' are believed to have originated. People did not know nor understand in those very early days what took place or what the residents, who lived on site, were attempting. Within three years, Marconi's closed the school, when it was realized they could continue their work directly from Chelmsford.

The Frinton Postmistress was Mrs Smith although one of her sons was also classified by residents and local Guide Books as the Postmaster. Albert

84

Smith was an inventor who amongst other things created a new Wireless Telegraphy Machine. This was produced during the years Marconi's School were working in Frinton, but there is no indication as to whether Marconi ever looked or listened to what Smith had to offer. It has been suggested that the founder of the Company, Marconi, used one of the houses after the School closed, and there is even mythology of his 'creating the wireless there', but neither visits nor his experiments in the House can be confirmed.

As Frinton grew, so did the number of people living within the community. The present primary school was built in 1914 at a cost of £1800, to take between 120 and 150 pupils, and there were eventually five Private schools in the Town. One of these was a girls school started in 1921 by Miss Edith Regge at Hawthornes. Nine years later she added, Glencoe, which another lady had been running as a private school.

During the war, the girls were all evacuated to Shropshire, and on their return, Hillcrest, which pre-war had been the Boys Private School, did not re-open, so Miss Regge took this over during the last years her school was to continue. The girls during the Tennis Tournements were employed at a shilling a day as Ball Girls. At Hawthornes they had their own Girl Guide Troop but it was only for those that attended Miss Regge's School, and no other girls were allowed to join.

As had happened in Walton, when Brannon had tried to create a new community, so too in Frinton, when it was announced in 1926 that 200 acres had been bought between Walton and Frinton, but nothing was done to the area and it was resold in 1934 and that a large number of houses were visualised. 1100 homes, a School, Cinema, Shops, Churches and a seafront Hotel. So began the saga of Frinton Park Estates attempt to create a new Town in between Walton and Frinton.

In 1929 it had been established that the Railway line to Walton was too close to the edge of the cliffs, and it was moved inland, passing through Pedlars Wood (in recent years this has become a Nature reserve under the capable hands of Pam Garrard) and the first train on the new track travelled to Walton in May 1930. Some houses on the original route have sleepers and even Rail Track still resting in their gardens.

It was about this time the 'The Lido' opened on the Greensward, by The Leas. Two buildings, with a Theatre, Resturant, coffee shop and Ice Cream Parlour and also an open air swimming pool. All the things that were similar to those seen in the South of France or in American films. The problem was that because of the continual subsidence and the pool being made only of concrete, it cracked, and it never held water after the first year.

Unfortunately it was at this time that there was the decrease in number of the 'in' crowd living, or wanting to live, in Frinton, and whilst initially, the well known visitors including Gracie Fields and Gladys Cooper went to events at The Lido, it was within five years to be put up for sale. It was immediately purchased by the South Coast Property Investment Company, and it was they who were planned their grandiouse scheme which was to be a completly 'modern' estate. The Lido was not considered suitable, and it was knocked down.

South Coast Properties had plans for a complete town of Art Deco houses that were, even in 1935, to be classified as 'Ultra Modern'. Many with curved walls. A Round House. They were to be designed by the very prominent Oliver Hill and his team of nineteen Architects.

There are many reasons why the Estate did not progress and the forthcoming war in 1939 is often quoted as the reason, but this was not correct. A typical attitude regarding these 'new' houses, was one viewer in 1936 stating that he was horrified to find 'that the Toilet was by the front door'. This seems a strange attitude today, but sixty years ago, this was just one aspect which ensured people were turning them down.

When the land was purchased, the potentials for the Estate were outstanding. From 1935, after the Prince of Wales and the camp followers had left the area, things were radically altered and the type of people that would have bought these modern Houses, were moving elsewhere.

The major mistake with the Frinton Park Estate was it built only very 'modern' homes. Had the conventional styles been built, the growth of this 'new' town could have grown and continued, but those which were built were far too modern for the type of people that were then coming to Frinton. The dream became a nightmare. A block of shops was opened with a Baker, dressmaker and a wool shop, but within ten months they had closed through lack of business, and Frinton Park Court, on the edge of

Pedlers Wood, is now partially used as a Masonic Hall, and with no preservation order, in 1994, the rest of the building is a disgrace.

Of the 1100 homes due to be built, only 32 were completed, and as the roads are still privately owned there is still no street lighting and the streets and the bridge over the Railway are in a very poor state of repair.

Chapter 8   TRAVELLING

The Romans created the first roads, with the Military Road, between Colchester and London amongst the first. As Harwich developed as a shipping port, the road from Colchester was extended as it was also to Ipswich and to Norwich as they grew in size. The track from Kirby to Walton, was never a road, but simply worn and established with the continual use of man. The nearest Town was Thorpe, where the Lawyers, Doctors and business's flourished. Some workers and their families moved from village to village. Others remained in one place all their lives. As long as they had a home and their Ale they were happy. They heard of the wonders of the big cities but seldom stirred from where lived and worked. Few in those far off days would have managed to even get to Thorpe as seldom did they own any form of transport. The rich had their carriages and their horses. They had the time and the money to go further afield.

In the 1600's it was realized people were willing to pay money to travel. Bullocks were attached to waggons and it took days to get anywhere. Average speed of six miles a hour, and seldom people travelled at night. The 1600's changed to the 1700's. Horses replaced the Bullocks, and the Stagecoach became a reality, although it wasn't until McAdam's system of road building was to cover the Country that the Stage increased it's reliablity, but with better roads, so too better Stagecoachs. Horses were stabled along their routes to enable fast changes and less stopping time.

The Postal service became organised and with it the Mail Coaches which all contractors vied to attain. Speedier transport and the whole country covered.

All of this happened initially between major towns, but sleepy Kirby, Gt.

Holland and Walton having no major routes leading anywhere, were to remain fairly static until the 1820's. As Walton developed as a seaside resort, so a Stage service was offered by Isaac Moles. He would await the arrival of the London Coach at the Red Lion in Colchester, and, taking the bags of those wishing to go to Walton, he would walk them to the George Hotel, which was the starting point of the Walton Horsebus. This was basically an open topped Horse drawn cart and available only three days a week

Walton had started to grow with the completion of the Pier in 1830, and with the second Pier this ensured that Walton could expand even more, and it was still being improved in 1905 when this Pier had a berth built to accomodate three Boats at a time, yet by this time the railways were taking far more passengers and the Boats were carrying less people each year.

It was in 1840 that the rail link between London and Colchester was completed, although for the first three years it was used only to carry freight. Only in 1843 were the first passengers to be carried. The Walton Horsebus was to continue it's passenger service but they still collected and delivered people only on those same three days that they had linked with the Stagecoach, and it wasn't until Robert Cresswell took over the route, that a daily service (excepting Sundays) was begun throughout the season, and then this was to be increased to twice a day, with Cresswell driving the 'Bus' personally. He changed horses at the Black Boy in Weeley, prior to taking it onto Kirby and the passengers had their first glimpse of the Sea.

The first moves to extend the Railway towards Walton took place when a link from Colchester to Harwich was built in 1854. Bruff being a Railway Engineer had the vision to see that the Railways were a great potential money spinner in bringing people to Walton and it was he that was to devise the route from Colchester.

Slowly it became a reality when it reached Hythe and then Wivenhoe. At this point two alternative rail links to Walton were suggested. One to travel through Weeley or the other through Mistley, which would then link up with the Harwich Trains, but it would take people down to Thorpe and onto

88

Walton. Eventually the cost factor was seen to disadvantage the latter scheme. The rail link was eventually to reach Weeley on 8th January 1866 and Kirby Cross by 26th July 1866, with Thorpe as an intermediate station. It reached Walton on the 17th May 1867, and for many years Walton's first Station Master, Robert Scott was to meet every one of the four trains from Colchester daily.

The original site proposed for Walton Station was by Newgate Street, but in retrospect, with Bruff's involvement, it can be seen he didn't want it other than where it is now, as it was then central for the properties he rented out to visitors.

Bruff then tried to arrange a Rail link between Clacton and Thorpe, but this was rejected as there was no Town at that time at what is now Clacton. Bruff also suggested a direct link to Harwich from Walton and this was started but stopped as Bruff found his funds diminishing.

Whilst he had managed to complete the Pier at Clacton, it wasn't until July 1882 that a rail link to this new Town was completed. Until that time, Walton had benifited. Between July and October 1882, nearly 50,000 Excursion tickets to Walton were sold on both the Railways and the Boats. That August Bank Holiday people had to obtain beds in Kirby, as Walton was full.

It can be seen that once the Railtrack had been laid to Clacton and with what Bruff was doing to the Town, it was bound to have an effect on Walton's visitor levels. The railway had lowered the number of people on the Boats, and whilst there was a daily service before the first World War, when the Steamers restarted in 1919, they were never to be as effective as they had been. Generally from then on they either stopped running, or amalgamated with others and then stopped!

There was a proposal to create a rail spur at Thorpe to enable holiday-makers to travel directly between Clacton and Walton, which would again have benifited Bruff, but this was also rejected.

A station was built at Kirby Cross, but not at Frinton, although first class passengers could request being let off where the Gates are at this time.

1st Class passengers could also hail the Train at Frinton to get onto it. Richard Stone III with his two daughters were the first at Frinton to use this system. It wasn't until 1888, that a station was built, but still for a number of years, fast trains to Walton did not stop at Frinton, unless a first class passenger requested it to.

On the day the Station was opened at Frinton, there were 15 people booked, yet 25 got off. The Tendring Hundred Railway owners and Directors were amongst those disembarking. They were met by William Bailey, who had been brought in for a short period to act as Station Master. The Directors were then transported to the Queens Hotel for lunch. In 1882 Walton Station had it's first refreshment room added, and Frinton was also to have one within a few years. Goods sidings were to be found by all three stations, enabling a service for goods to be carried by Train.

In August 1881 a Railway line between Walton and Harwich was proposed again but as had happened previously, it was the lack of finances that stopped this progressing beyond new plans that had been drawn up by Phillip Brannon.

As roads became better, land transport grew in scope and in 1894 the first motor Car was seen in Walton. Both Col. Davis of the Dairy, and Robert Robinson Snr. tossed a coin to see who would have the first short journey in it. Col. Davis won.

As the visitors grew in number, many desired a memento of their journey. Rickarby the Towns chemist in Walton had perfume named OCEANIDES on sale, with a label showing a Sea Nymph and an etching of Walton, and in his shop window he utalised the wordage that the bottles should be purchased as a 'gift for friends as a memory of your visit'. It was in the 1880's that German Porcelain manufacturers were travelling to Britain offering cheap cups and saucers, vases and even moustache cups, which had a Black and White local view (transfers of etchings) on them. Within a few years these pictures were being produced in colour, and a range of pottery, with at least a dozen different views showing Walton before 1900, were available.

In the 1880's W H Goss started producing small models of varied historical items, which included small urns, vases, etc, and a crest or shield of the town where they were purchased. He started by offering these items

90

to the towns where the models had originally been found, or where they were seen in local Museums, but he soon discovered that all towns wanted these same models, but with 'their' own crest on them. He arranged salesmen to travel the country offering a growing number of models, and stating that if a Town did not have a Crest or a Shield, their team would create one. So it was that by 1900 Walton had a fine crest, and within five years, Frinton also.

What Goss started, so other manufacturers copied, and there were some fine makes including 'Arcadian' and 'Shelley', but standards diminished with German and the Czech companies also making the same type of item at greatly reduced costs. All manufacturers started copying Goss's Crests/Shields. Goss intimated that those he had created were his copyright, and so new Crests and Shields had to be devised and this is why today Frinton is known to have at least four different and Walton five. In Walton 'The Old Curiosity Shop' had a window full of Crested China in 1900 and Blowers and Cooper in Frinton were to have large stocks in later years.

The Goss Pattern Book showed they had prepared an illustrated picture of the Beach and promenade at Frinton to be reproduced on some of their larger pieces, but todate no example has been seen, so it is doubtful that it ever went further that the proposal stage. Neither Kirby nor Great Holland are known to have had any Crested China

Since these early days there has usually been some form of Holidayware available, but things have got out of hand when small potteries offer modern Thatched Cottages with the word Frinton written on them. It shows the makers and outlets ignorance, as there has never been a picture or print produced, which shows any such building within the town.

From the late 1920s there was a continual call for a Light Aircraft Aerodrome in Walton. The council in their wisdom continually turned this down, as they had rejected the proposal for a Tramway between Walton and Frinton in the 1870's, as it was seen as not being necassary. Even Alan Cobham's Flying Circus, who gave a display in the early 1930's, on fields between Frinton and Walton, still did not manage to make them change their minds.

An agreement in the 1980's was made to allow buses within the Gates at

91

Frinton. Powell Cooper had specified that this would not happen, and for years, the Omnibus's had travelled from Colchester and Clacton along the road to Walton, passing the Gates. Yet those with little vision rushed to get the buses agreement, as they stated it would bring more business into Frinton. They were aware through the letters pages of the local paper that the opposite would happen, and that buses would as easilly take people out of the Town, to shop cheaper elsewhere. Prior to the buses, Frinton shopkeepers had a captured elderly population, who, without transport, had to use the Connaught Avenue shops. Once the buses started, this ensured an even greater loss of business within Frinton, having, as indicated, the exact opposite effect to that which the shopkeepers had been advocating, ensuring that as numerous shops have been forced to close, it is doubtful that the 'Bond Street' of East Anglia will ever return to it's former glory.

Chapter 9 SCANDALS AND INTRIGUES

Good times are generally remembered, yet the bad are often forgotten. Occasionally, when situations produce the most newsworthy topicality of yesteryear, they are often repeated in books and articles but with time they change, as words and phrases are left out by writers when indicating the past, and the end results are then altered to make an event appear more interesting.

One story that makes good reading even if it actually happened elsewhere, and the main players had little to do with this area, it is a true story which can never be fully told, as it appears more complicated than that which was being stated even at the time.

'Murder most foul' is a phrase used in story books, but the murder of Martha Reay as she was leaving the Covent Garden Theatre on April 14th 1779 was just that. Martha Reay had been to see the play 'Love in a Village' when she was approached by the Rev. James Hackman who took out a pistol and shot her through the temple. Then with a second pistol, he tried to kill himself, but failed, missing and mortally wounding another, and then, crouching on the ground, and in a feeble attempt to kill himself, he started pummelling his skull with the pistol butt.

92

She was buried within two days, and three days later he was on trial at the Old Bailey. He was sentenced, convicted, and then hung within three weeks.

James Hackman had been in the Army, where his parents had bought him a commission in the 68th Regiment of Foot, but finding the life not to his calling, he decided to become a clergyman. Prior to leaving the Army he became part the entourage that Lord Sandwich had around him, after they met at a 'recruiting party'. From then on, he was caught up in what he saw as the glamour of the type of life they led, and so he often visited his Lordships home, and accompanied the group when they went to functions, the Theatre or were involved in private and public events together, even when, as often happens, he could ill afford to do so.

Amongst the party was Martha Reay (born 1745), who had been 'discovered' by Lord Sandwich at the age of 16, and, as was the situation in those days, he had taken her under his wing, and she had become his Mistress. She then provided him over the next eighteen years with nine children, of which four had died at birth.

It can be said, that Hackman was first and foremost a misguided 'innocent', because, although Lord Sandwich was to be made aware by his manservant that Miss Reay had taken Hackman to her bed, other than warning her to be more discrete, Hackman, even after he had left the Army and gone into the church, was still being invited to parties given by Lord Sandwich, suggesting that what Miss Reay did, without Sandwich either seeing or hearing, was accepted.

Because of his hopeless desire for Miss Reay, although Hackman had a church and been made it's curate, there is no record of him ever officiating at any services.

Miss Reay had been trained by Giardini, a leading voice Coach of the day, and was known to have a sweet voice, and it was 'musical to a high degree'. She was also taught at Sandwich's expense, elecution and deportment. Her portrait had been painted by Gainsborough. Yet when she was not with Lord Sandwich, she found friendship with those of the Theatre, and it was stated, £3000 was due to spent by her protector to set her on the stage.

Robert Rigby owned Mistley Hall as well as most of Kirby and Walton, and he regularly attended the functions which Sandwich arranged. Like too many of his class and of that period, he was a man who greatly enjoyed any number of pleasures, amongst which were wine and women, and, when he heard Miss Reay say she 'liked the Sea', he offered her space in the Trinity Tower on the Naze at Walton, which he suggested she use as her 'Tea Rooms'. He was able to do this, as he was the custodian of the Tower, through his ownership of Walton Hall, and could do so without Trinity Houses knowledge.

Accordingly, whenever she made the journey to Walton, she invited her Theatrical friends to join her. David Garrick is suppposed to have been a visitor on a number of occasions, but she also invited many ladies of the theatre, for she knew that Lord Sandwich's and Rigby's male friends would also attend without their wives, and the phrase 'pity she's a whore' was still being used during this period with regard to the young (and not so young) ladies of the theatre.

They all stayed at Walton Hall, which Rigby owned, and it is presumed, some were to 'sleep' in the Tower. It was suggested that Rigby, who owed money to many, was attempting to keep in with Sandwich, and it was Rigby who made all the arrangements and invited only those on Sandwich's lists of acceptable people, to stay at the Hall and to 'take Tea' at the Trinity Tower, although it is now surmised that the building was being used for other purposes than just drinking Tea and making polite conversation.

Yet within his own circle, Sandwich seemed remote to Miss Reay, and was known to speak harshly at functions to any of the Ladies or Gentlemen present if they tried to have a conversation with her. After the years as his Mistress, she had learnt to be seen, but remain silent, unless asked to sing by Sandwich. What Lady Sandwich thought of this arrangement has never been ascertained, although she must have been aware of the situation, often attending the same events as Miss Reay.

Unfortunately, Miss Reay, in her choice of Hackman as her lover, failed to understand that he would become more than simply infatuated with her, as he proposed marriage many times, to be rejected continually. She knew he could offer her little, whilst the 'old man', Sandwich, would ensure her well being, as well as their childrens future. Hackman continued to make

94

advances, entreat and plead with her, seeing in her only what he wished. He wrote numerous letters to her, stating that he liked and he was quite willing to take her children on, if she would marry him. What he did not see, was that he was one of a number of lovers she had, and that it is presumed, Sandwich knew about, and as such he accepted, by turning a blind eye to what she did.

Two hundred years later it is impossible to know what the actual circumstances of this relationship was, and based on comments in Diaries and letters then exisiting, it is very possible that Sandwich was well aware of the correspondence from Hackman to Miss Reay, and both he and his Mistress treated Hackman's adoration as an entertainment and a joke, and this was why Hackman was continually invited to events as part of the group, utalising him as the Court Jester, and to which Hackman was quite blind.

It was after being rejected again (and again), that Hackman followed her to London after they had all stayed one weekend in Walton. He waited outside Covent Garden Theatre, and when she left, he saw Lord Sandwich's Coach arrive. At the Trial, one of the witness's stated it was Lady Sandwich's carriage, presumably to try and ensure that no scandel would follow. One of the party, Lord Colerine, who was accompanying her, held her hand, to lead her into the Carriage, and it was here that Hackman, believing that the man who took her hand was a lover (and probably was), in a fit of jealousy and rage, stepped from behind a pillar, and killed her.

The major argument in court was that it was not a spontaneous decision, and that he must have gone to the Theatre with the thought of killing her, because he was carrying two pistols. Normally in those times, gentlemen carried one, to ward off the cut throats of that period. It was his carrying two that ensured he received the death penalty. Many people who knew them both and the background, were to exclaim that he should have received only a short sentence, because of the 'torment' they knew she had led him.

What ensured the story was to be repeated, and often wrongly, was Sir Herbert Croft wrote a satirical story, called 'Love and Madness' in which he wrote a series of love letters purporting to have been written between Reay and Hackman. Although neither their real names, nor Sandwich's were used, everyone in society was aware to whom the references were pointing, and his fiction became accepted as fact, especially when the book went into at least ten different printings over the next ten years. Sandwich was made a laughing stock.

Reading a complete transcript of the Trial which was held on the 19th April 1779, it is interesting to note that at no time throughout the proceedings, which lasted less than a day, was Lord Sandwich's name mentioned. Only four witness's were called, and Hackman announced his guilt. Lord Sandwich's wifes carriage was indicated, but simply that it was picking up the party of people after they had been to the Theatre. It was Sir Herbert Crofts book that was to do the damage, and Tea Parties were never held in the Walton Tower again.

In 1843 a man quarrelled with his wife in Gt. Holland, and whilst drunk, threw a knife at her, which ended in her side. She died that night and the doctor examining decided that it was not the knife that had killed her. Her neighbours, knowing the victim, stressed her death came about 'through too much excitment and violent passion'!

Another story that is always worth reading is that of Kitty Canham, who married the Vicar of Thorpe in 1845, and after leaving him, bigamously married John Primrose, Lord Dalmeny. On her deathbed she requested she be returned to Thorpe to be buried. Both husbands attended her burial service. There are suggested links with Kirby in this story, because the Vicar also officiated there (and at Walton) but other than this very tentative link, this is really a Thorpe story that should be left as such for others to tell, yet one Walton story of love and intrigue is that of the smuggler, Captain Palmer and his daughter Lucy.

Like all good fables, the dates become confused, because the story suggests that part of Walton Church fell into the Sea on the 23rd December 1798, which could represent the truth, if a section of the walling did go to the Sea such a short time after the roof of the Church had given way that same year.

Yet the story will be repeated here in as much detail as it was quoted in 1871.

Captain Palmer lived between Walton and Frinton, on a farm, of which the actual farming was little, for Palmers main activity was Smuggling. He dealt with the Dutch, who came over frequently with Gin, Brandy, Tea and Tobacco.

Palmers wife had died when their daughter Lucy was 14. Lucy Palmer was aware of her fathers activities, but she had little influence over him and he had started bringing the Dutch 'traders' to the house after the wifes death, for until she had died, he had not been allowed to bring any of the smugglers into the home.

Captain Palmer spoke Dutch, and, when the 'visitors' came they always did their dealings in this language, so Lucy was normally ignorant of what was being spoken. Only a few of those that visited spoke some English. One of these, a Michael Tromp, became a regular visitor.

Basically Lucy wasn't happy with her father continually bringing these Dutchmen home. It made life difficult, and she would as often as possible visit her mothers relatives living in Beaumont, where she was befriended by a lad named Richard Salmon. This friendship soon developed and turned into love.

She became aware at about this time that Tromps visits were getting more frequent and her father kept leaving them together. On one occasion her father told her in advance that Tromp was coming and that she should wear her prettiest dress. She realized from his words and actions, her father had agreed that Tromp could propose marriage to her. This she did not want, so when he arrived, she was wearing her oldest and dirtiest clothes, and yet, when the opportunity was there, Tromp, with her fathers insistance, followed Lucy into the back kitchen and in halting English stated he loved her and wished to marry her.

During the period Tromp had been visiting the house, Lucy had grown to dislike the man and his crude ways. The way he looked at her, and even his touch, and so she replied as she felt and left the kitchen and went to her bedroom, where she bolted the door.

Her father followed her up the stairs and shouted at the bedroom door that he had decided she would become Tromps wife and she would be married on Christmas Day. To pacify her father, she told him through the door, which she would not open, that to be married she would need a new bonnet and a new scarf, and her father left the house to join Tromp on the beach and tell him what he thought was the good news regarding the marriage, believing that her words indicated an acceptance, unaware that his daughter was gathering everything she could and was to leave the house as quickly as possible, escaping and going to Beaumont and her relatives.

So far we have a tale of the wicked father and the pure and innocent daughter. Yet everything was to change over the next few hours, when Lucy met up with Richard Salmon and he agreed to take Lucy back to her home, with a small cart, so she could get the rest of her belongings. He suggested, with his mothers approval, that Lucy should then become part of the Salmons household.

The weather had turned and yet Lucy knew her father would not be at home with a boat to be unloaded, and she and Richard set out for the Palmer Farm. As they approached the farmhouse there was in the distance, a massive sound of land and buildings falling into the water from within the Walton area, and Lucy instinctively knew that it involved her father, for she was aware they had been using the old buildings by the Church to store the contraband.

Captain Palmer had been with Tromp, off loading the Brandy and other items, and they had placed the gold Palmer was paying for the goods, into one of the coffins within the Cemetary around the original Church that had become exposed through erosion. This ensured they could all manhandle the goods from the boat quickly.

As they were nearing the last of these trips from the beach the land must have given way, and as it was a rough and stormy night, they were swept out to Sea. Indications suggested there must have been a fight as they tried to save themselves, and the bodies which turned up some days later showed human teeth marks on Tromps fingers, suggesting that he had clung onto Palmer, who had used his teeth to break the grip.

Whatever had happened is unknown, but the empty Boat in the water and no sign of the two men or the crew, and with a part of the buildings having gone, Lucy was certain they had to be dead as her father had been a very strong swimmer. Richard Salmon rushed her back to his home, as he felt it wrong she should be left alone under these circumstances.

Some months later, after seeing Richard everyday, whilst she continued to stay at his home in Beaumont, their love blossomed and he proposed

98

marriage. They spent hours together and on one occasion, he took her in a boat for a row along the Coastline. Whilst they were crossing the area where the land had slipped into the sea, and where her father had perished, the water was low and the rubble from the buildings and the cliffs were below the boat, when their oar struck what felt like solid wood. It was possibly a coffin, and Richard knowing he could use the wood, decided to wait whilst the Tide went out further. Eventually a coffin did appear, but as it was of some weight, Richard got out of the boat and removed the lid to discover not only Gold, but also some papers wrapped in oilskins, which transpired to be letters from Michael Tromp to her father. They had actually discovered her fathers payment to Tromp.

Lucy was overjoyed, but she decided that she could no longer live so close to where her father had died, and so, once Richard and Lucy were married, the two of them, plus Mrs Salmon (her husband, the local Doctor, having died some years earlier) all went to live in Canada.

Fables and fantasies abound, and this is possibly one of them. Had the gold been found and hidden by the two youngsters when they realized that Palmer and Tromp were missing? Did the two men fight because of the land slippage, or were they fighting before it happened, over the daughter? Nobody will know, but it makes a good 'Walton' story.

There are a few 'tales' that seem more versed in fiction than fact, but these have been set to one side, so that, if at some point in the future, more details come to hand, then they may possibly be reserected and used. Ghosts are mentioned but these are not worth repeating as they are generally figments of someones imagination. The sound of the 'Ghostly Bells' of the original Church has little essence in truth.

The Church is supposed to have risen out of the Sea in January 1928, but as the building fell, wall by wall, and piece by piece and a lot was dismantled to assist in the foundations of the new Church, it is very unlikely Father Neptune would have been able to do a rebuild job based on the rubble on the Sea floor. What appeared was no more than materials from the Church, and probably other buildings as well, at a spot, opposite the Pier Hotel, about halfway along the side of the Pier as it was in the 1920's (the present Pier being shorter now). Nothing more.

Who was Cornelious a Tilbury? It is stated that this man was being included within prayers and thanksgiving into the late 1750's, 'because he had eaten a large amount of poison and survived'. According to Holmes Notes, he was classified as a Frinton Farmer, but no biographical books indicate anything about him. Holmes states he lived between 1680 and 1720. Was he simply someone who gave the church money to give thanks for his escape, and that following Vicars automatically included him within their prayers, even after he had died from old age? There is no way now of knowing.

One story that was repeated for many years, was an eye witness account of a young woman who committed suicide in Walton, and because the Rev. Cooke refused to give the burial service, it was held at midnight, and the words were spoken by the Vicars wife. It was attended by most of the ladies of the Parish. Who she was is now forgotten, and the reasons for the refusal are also lost in time. Was it simply the fact she committed suicide that created a difficulty in the Vicars eyes and he considered she had committing a mortal sin in the eyes of God. Whatever the reason, this was yet another aspect of the congregations dislike for their Vicar during those years.

Chapter 10   SPORTS AND PERSONALITIES

Although it can be truthfully stated that it was Tennis and Golf that assisted in the development of Frinton, it had been Wildfowling and Fishing that originally created the trend to try and draw people to Walton and to Frinton, as publicity for both places before 1890 expounded the potentials awaiting the visitors in the Backwaters and in the Sea.

It wasn't until the 1840's, as the doors of Walton opened wider to an increasing flow of visitors, that the need was seen to give them more than just the sands, but also to entertain them as well.

There had been Fairs and Circus's attending Walton for two or three days at a time. Many of whom moved onto Gt. Holland or Kirby for the night or had come from there the previous day. One Steam Fair in the 1880's was reprimended for making too much noise, and in 1861 it was noted that Cookes Circus arrived having not only Horses, but an Elephant as well.

It was at the small Theatres in both the Pier and the Marine Hotels that Music Hall artistes started to appear. Henry Irving, before he was Knighted, visited and gave his solo performance on at least two occasions, but based on the small number of names that are mentioned in the local newspapers, the entertainment was generally performed by dozens of mediocre Ventriloquists, Magicians and entertainers. They appeared at either Dorlings Palace of Varieties (The Marine Hotel) or the Clifton Music Hall (The Pier Hotel), from the 1860's onwards.

These were small intimate theatres which offered sufficient room for locals and visitors alike throughout the season, and as the years progressed, an occasional singer and a lot of local entertainment were always on offer at these two venues, even during the winter months.

It was in the early 1860's that the town became very crowded one weekend when it was announced that the famous French tightrope walker Blondin would walk from the end of the Pier to a Boat moored some a distance away. A short time previously Blondin had made his third crossing on a tightrope over the Niagara Falls in Canada (in 1855, 1859 and 1860), carrying a man, wheeling a wheelbarrow and making the crossing blindfold.

Just the thought of such daring created excitement and awe, and Blondin was a man everyone wanted to see.

Handbills were distributed in the suburbs of London and the crowds flocked to Walton. Unfortunately nobody bothered to check with the man himself, as he was appearing in the North of England at the time, for it had been practical joker Charles Simpson of Sudbury who had set this up, using his friend, a local Sudbury printer to produce the handbills. The crowds started to become ugly when Blondin didn't appear, and things were made worse when many were unable to get home that night and they had to sleep on the beaches. The Town Cryer had to continually traverse the Town, ringing his bell and stating that 'Mr. Blondin regrets not being able to make the attempt - because he has hurt his big Toe!'

The Pier eventually had the Pavilion Theatre, which started with 400 seats, and was enlarged to seating seven hundred and fifty people. Even then with a larger premises available, few of the Music Hall Artistes appearing were really 'top of the bill'. Over the years, when an occasional headliner did appear, it was either as they were on their way up, or too often, on their way down.

Initially, during the 1800's, visitors coming to Walton, had been the 'well to to do' and towards the end of this era it had included the poet, Christina Rossetti, who stayed a few days in Walton in 1880, but she wasn't over impressed, indicating that 'Walton is a fairly agreeable place, yet I do not know whether I have a dislike for the surroundings'. Such comments were also being made elsewhere at that time. Two years later, a newspaper stated that Walton had 'The shabbiness of the respectability of age. Public spirit seems dead and buried, and it could have migrated to Clacton'. In 1878 it was stated 'It is not greatly distinguished or insufficiently vulger'

Yet a full description of Walton seven years before this remark, in 1871, suggests a truer perspective of times past. Whilst concentration and money was being spent on the 'new' Town, or it may be considered, 'Bruffs Town' the old part was 'most unsatisfactory. Untrapped privies are common. Pigs are kept in the back yards. Stagnent ditches are filled with black mud. Swarms of gnats and flies everywhere. At the rear of the 'Bath House' are heaps of Oyster Shells and manure accumulated. By the building there is a urinal built of wood, with a wooden floor, without drainage or water. Water throughout the Town is totally unfit for drinking. The Watering of Streets is badly done, and the residents are extremely poor'. It can be imagined the smell when it was hot, and why the council were to consider the needed sewage and drainage plan.

During this period a plague of rats was spread throughout both the new and old Town, and the Council arranged that although there was an official Rat Catcher, a fee would be paid for 'rats tails', and this developed into a money earner for the very poor, when a farthing (a quarter of a penny) a tail was paid. Twenty years later, during another period when rats were running the town, the cost of living had altered, and the figure rose to a half penny and thirty years later it rose to 2d a Tail in hope that this would eradicate them for good. It did not, for a few of their relatives are still around.

Daniel Defoe, the author of 'Robinson Crusoe', had come for a day, a

102

hundred and sixty years earlier (in 1722/3), whilst writing his 'Grand Tour of Britain'. John Constables son Alfred left after a few days in 1832, when he had produced few watercolours in a sketch pad. One Landscape was sold seperately, and the remaining pad made £2000 in Auction in 1993. His father never made the journey, although many books incorrectly state that he did. A very interesting painting by Ford Maddox Brown showing Walton in 1859 was originally sold for £84, and this now hangs in the Birmingham Art Gallery. J. Hassell was to paint the Walton Lifeboat at Sea on at least two seperate occasions.

It was Frinton that was to attract the well known names of stage and cinema. Up until the end of the first World War (1918) it had been just the rich, with many businessmen finding Frinton the perfect Seaside retreat. Amongst these were a few millionares, and all found Frinton in those early days to have a genteel atmosphere. Generally they came for no more than a few weeks, and being the monied classes, whilst a few homes were empty out of season, others had full time staff throughout the year.

One classic story in the early 1920's was of a family arriving a few days earlier than originally expected, to find the staff were not in their quarters, but sitting in the main dining room, enjoying their lunch. The owner hearing their voices in the dining room, opened the sliding doors. The Butler rose. The rest sat in silence. Their employer looked and closed the doors without saying a word. There were six employed full time, including the Butler, a Gardener, a Cook and three other staff, and yet the family never came to Frinton except for just four, or at most, five weeks each year.

The Butler was called into the study, and the household accounts were requested. He was then asked, in a voice that echoed around the house: 'Twenty Pounds of Butter - A week?'. Of course the Butler had been adding noughts to the accounts. The Employer immediately fired all the staff, and called on Tomkins (of Tomkins, Homer and Ley, the House Agents) within the hour. He then stated he wished to move to a slightly smaller house, and when Tomkins indicated that 'he would put the present house on the market', he was told, 'I do not want it on the market. I wish to sell today. I wish to buy today. I wish to move today. What have you got. If you cannot assist, I shall go elsewhere'. The outcome was that within 24 hours they were moved from 2nd Avenue, to another house in 3rd Avenue.

103

Money talked. Their daughter remembered those two days vividly.

Good things were being mentioned within 'Society' about Frinton, for it had something few other resorts could provide. Relaxation. Quiet. Golf and Tennis. It was in 1920 that it started to offer that which no place anywhere in the world could hope to contend with, for it was here that Royalty were to visit. In that year, Prince Edward, the Prince of Wales, travelled to Frinton, and stayed with a member of Frinton's Tennis Club Committee. From then on, and over the next fifteen years, both he and his brother Prince George, became regular visitors.

Even their mother, Queen Mary, came to look Frinton over, as her sons were continually returning throughout the 1920's.

Edwards visits were soon being made in the company of his good friend Mrs Douglas Ward, but this changed and visits became enhanced when Mrs Wallace Simpson took a house in Frinton, and she and Edward could meet without the prying eyes of the Press or public. Anything Edward or George did in Frinton was considered no more than Royalty 'having a fling', and a blind eye was turned whenever anything involved either of the Princes. Again the respect they both evolved, few people still living, even now, will talk about them.

It was this factor that created the 'exclusive' tag, for not only were there wealthy in abudance clammering to buy houses 'within the Gates', but those with their ear to the ground, spread the word, and this brought the select upper strata of the Theatrical Profession, as well as the 'bright young things', who all considered that Frinton was the place to be. It became the 'in' venue throughout the Season, especially as members of the Theatre found they could relax, without autograph hunters and fans pestering them.

Mrs Buckmaster, known Internatinally as Gladys Cooper, a true lady of the theatre and whose face adorned Chocolate Boxes and hundreds of postcards, was already living in Frinton. She was joined by the Dare sisters, both Zena and Phyllis. All three were friends, and were known as 'Beauties of the English Stage'. Gladys Cooper went eventually to America where she appeared on stage and in many movies ('My Fair Lady', etc). Her daughter Joan, went to school in Frinton, married Robert Morley, and their son Sheridan Morley is now an important writer on the Theatre and

104

Cinema. Gladys Coopers husband will always be remembered because it was he that invented the drink, the 'Bucks Fizz'

Gracie Fields used to come and visit her sister, who had the house 'Tinkerbell' on the corner of Greenway and Connaught Avenue. 'Our Gracie' appeared at benifits and fund raising at the Imperial Hall, and was often seen visiting shows at the LIDO. Dame Clara Butt, whose voice was heard in most homes in Britain, on 78 rpm recordings, was to be joined over the next twenty years by nearly every leading personality of the British Theatre and Cinema. Some came for weekends. Others took houses for the Season.

Douglas Fairbanks Snr and his Third wife arrived in their Yacht, which was left a short distance from Frinton's Beach, and they first stayed with Gladys Cooper. They rented a house and Fairbanks Junior played at the Tennis Club and Senior worked out daily on parallel bars erected in the garden of the house.

Even Amy Johnson is supposed to have flown in, and landed at the Golf Club. The list of names is long. Too long, but think of any 'star' of the twenties (and early thirties), from Jessie Mathews to Jack Buchanan, and including Noel Coward, Ivor Novello, George Bernard Shaw and writer Edgar Wallace, and the majority visited or stayed in Frinton at one time or another during the period 1920 to 1935.

When Prince Edward and Mrs Simpson left, so did the Theatricals. In recent years resident Jack Watling, with all of his Theatrical family, have been part of the Frinton scene. After the war Ann Todd and Derek Farr and a decreasing number of Cinema faces arrived for Tennis Week, but the heyday of Frinton, once able to draw the big names, was past. The South of France called the 'young things' after the Royalty stopped visiting Frinton by the mid 1930's, and now with modern Air Travel, the world is their oyster, but during those heady years, Frinton saw Winston Churchill and his son Randolph. Ramsey MacDonald and other ministers, as well as Von Ribbontrop the German Ambassador prior to the 1939/45 War (whose German staff were spying on the area). Both Prince Michael of Jugoslavia and King Zog of Albania with his wife Queen Charlotte stayed during the war years, and the Emperor of Abyssinia took over a house for some months during this period.

Prince Edward enjoyed Frinton because he could play both Golf and Tennis without the crowds following and gawping. Neither of these two sports did Frinton any harm, for it was Royalty that ensured the top names came to play, as they often met Prince Edward, especially at the Tennis Club, where he asked to be treated like everyone else and assisted in mowing the Lawns and working behind the bar, as all members did in those days.

Sport has always been part of the life of most Villages throughout the Country. In Walton in 1614 people involved in building a Sea Wall were known to have played 'Footballe' and in the 1800's all Villages had Cricket and Football teams, although it was some years before Frinton could gather enough players. Both sports were to be played on the Greensward until the Frinton teams obtained their own grounds. The MCC were to play Frinton regularly during the 1920's and 1930's.

Cricket was being played in Walton on Bath House Meadow in 1878, and the Walton Cricket Club was started the following year. Kirby had a team for very many years, but they didn't become an Association until 1931. Local Cricketers even had a regular one (half) day match every year on Gunfleet Sands during the 1920's.

In Walton the 'Regatta' became an important event within the Town, when from about 1820, local teams took part in various Rowing and Sailing races. In 1834, Benjimin Kent suggested they start inviting teams from other Towns to take part. Already great crowds were being drawn to this aquatic event, and in 1833 over 2000 people had attended. When teams from Felixstowe, Harwich, Clacton and Southend took part, this number rose dramatically.

In the first 'open' event, Walton produced a close win in the four man rowing event, with W Polley, W. Smith, J Cole and T Simey in their boat 'Viper' beating teams from Ipswich and Harwich. People stood on the shore or promenade, or were quite willing to pay well above the normal admission price, to stand and watch from the Pier. (6d as oppossed to a 1d or 2d)

Regetta Day from the 1840's was to end with an added attraction. A fine Firework Display put on regularly by Mr. Brock of Crystal Palace fame,

106

and then in later years by Mr Pain, renowned for his displays at Alexandra Palace. As the years progressed the event was to become known as the 'Regatta and Land Sports Annual Event'. Swimming was added to the water sports.

Land events initially took place on the green in front of the Marine Hotel, and then they moved to the Bathhouse Meadow, with Donkey Derby's and greasy Poles to climb. Athletics and Tug of War, and what had taken one day, became two, as varied sports and entertainments were added. Another Regatta was started in 1879 as an alternative, and organised by the Watermen, but this, like so many things, disappeared when the war started in 1914, and was not to return afterwards.

Memories of the Regatta are few. A Barge arriving from Maldon with over a hundred people on board and a Band playing. In 1834 after the event had finished, the 'Hero Coach' returning to Colchester overturned and a number of people were injured.

The Ipswich Packet sold special tickets for the Regatta in 1835, and they had a band, the 'Ipswich Militia', that played on board the ship throughout most of the day. For a few years there was even a floating pontoon for people to sit and watch closer to the events, and those using this seated area, paid not only for their seats, but also to be helped (or even carried) to and from the Pontoon so they did not get their feet wet.

The highlight for many was attending a function held in a large tent attached to the Marine (Kents) Hotel, when winners prizes were given out. A fine meal was served and many Toasts were drunk and afterwards, there was always a Ball in the Hotel, with sixty or seventy of the 'best people'.

The Regatta's history after the first World War was changable. It restarted and then for eight years it stopped. It began again in the early 1930's, and continued up until the start of the second world war. It was some time before the Regatta restarted during the post-war years, and it has now become part of the RNLI's fund gathering. In 1967 an annual Carnival Parade was started as a Charity fund raiser.

Swimming eventually was an integral part of the Regatta, and in 1893 Walton became affiliated to the Amatuer Swimming Association. Water Polo was also introduced as part of water Sports and Walton remained unbeaten at home for many years.

A popular sport for the 'well to do' in the early days of Walton was Croquet, but this changed when, at the back of the Marine Hotel, they opened a Tennis Court in 1876. With Mrs Crossley as their secretary, a perminent site in Vicarage Gardens was agreed in 1878, and it was then that Walton began it's Lawn Tennis Club.

In Frinton, in early 1900, Mrs Franklin decided that using her neighbours, the Bevingtons Tennis court was fun, but it was too small as it became more popular, and a club with courts was needed. With a committee which included Viscount Horncastle, they purchased and leased some land, and on the 29th December 1900 opened the 'Frinton Tennis, Croquet and Bowls Club'.

Croquet was still being played at the Frinton Club until the 1970's when it was decided to close the Lawns and build a swimming pool and add some Squash Courts. Bowls were started in 1901, but they were played for only a few seasons. The club would have been the oldest in the area, had it continued, but as it was, Walton opened a Bowls Club at the Round Gardens in 1908, making them the oldest continually playing Team in the Tendring League. Their site was closed in 1929 when they decided to move across the road, as the banking around the Round Gardens created a situation where it occasionally become waterlogged and some matches had to be cancelled. They had not been given an official 'competition playing area' acceptance by the League because of this. A club in Frinton opened besides the Queens Hotel on the Esplanade, and was to move twice before reaching it's present home. At one time, there were two clubs in Frinton. There were Bowls Clubs in both Kirby and Gt. Holland.

Although Frinton and Walton had their main Tennis Clubs, there were still other courts in the area. The club house at Frinton was purchased during the time when they altered their changing rooms, and the Club House was to become a large thatched building. The original building had been in use between 1901 and 1927, and then it was shifted to a new club that then had started in Kirby, at the Playing Fields, These grounds had been purchased for them by Sir Joseph Hood of Frinton. It was stated that the old Cricket Ground at Kirby was 'like a ploughed field most of the time', prior to the change.

They started Archery at the Frinton Club in the 1920's but this did not continue as few were interested. Archery was restarted again in the early 1950's, but as before, this did not last more than a year or two. Squash rackets were begun at Frinton in 1946.

Throughout the period before and then immediately after the first world war, Quoits were being played in competitions. Walton won the Challenge Shield many times, and one player from Gt. Holland often won the event. Horse riding was also popular especially as there were many ex-Military in Frinton. The East Essex and Suffolk Hounds hunted the district.

The Walton Volunteers (the Territorials of yesteryear) had an 800 yard Rifle Range on the Naze, which they opened on the 28th July 1880. This was then reduced to 400 yards in 1905. Once the gentry had decimated nearly every bird within the Backwaters, including everything from Swans to Robins, many transfered their shooting skills to competitions. Soon there were three Rifle Clubs who used the range and each had a number of different teams. The Course was extended back to 800 yards when there was talk of war in 1914, but after the war finished, the Range did not re-open.

In Frinton, Powell Cooper set about leasing a large section of Holland Marshes in 1895, which he had drained and landscaped. The only thing the Marshes had previously been used for, was Hare Coursing and sheep farming and although the work had not been completed, Frinton Golf Course was to open in 1896. It had been designed by Tom Dunn and initially it had five nine hole Courses, and within two years, over 200 members. With the realization that an 18 hole course was required, the layout was altered by Willie Park in 1903. There were even two six hole courses for Children by 1909. The course was then redesigned again in 1929 by H S Colt, but throughout the changes, one nine hole was to remain for the use of the Ladies.

A Club House was built in Third Avenue in 1898, and at one time the first Tee started on the Greensward. Second Avenue did not exist, but then in 1903 the Club House was moved to where it now stands, and it was also enlarged. A long strip of land was to be sliced off the side of the Golf Course and sold as plots for house building. This created Second Avenue, or as it was later known 'Millionaires Road'. The first club coach was W H Webb, who wrote a 1/- (one shilling) paperback volume on Golf in 1902.

Prince Edward assisted the Golf Club in Frinton unknowingly, for the club grew in statue, really on his back, with the Ryder Cup team playing for a few years during the 1920's and into the 1930's. Many leading International players visiting Britain were also to make the trip to the Frinton Links, but with the advent of war, and the decreasing number of personalities in Frinton, it has ensured the course is now used predominently by the locals.

A Golf Club was started at the Naze in 1928. James Braid who had been British Champion four times designed it. Within two years the club had over 800 members. E A Alexandra, whose brainchild the club had been, had financial problems in 1938, and he went into Bankruptcy. At that point there were 1200 members and it had a fine Club House which had been built by the Trinity Landmark. The course was laid by Charlie Grey, who had been at the Frinton Club, and Walton's First Coach, Charlie Bright had originally been the assistant Coach at Frinton.

When the Club closed there was an immediate attempt by members to restart it, but war began and it wasn't until late 1945 that a new call to reopen the course was made. The problem was clearing the live mines and ammunition, plus the shrapnel the war had left behind, and it was during this time, in 1946, whilst the Army were clearing the site that the Club House was struck by lightening and it burnt down. It was then realized that through the continual erosion the Naze was a lot smaller than it had been before the war, and it really had become quite dangerous for players. It was this that ensured it was not to reopen.

Frintons yearly Tennis Tournement drew every major player in Tennis between 1910 and up until the 1970's. Mrs Austin and Perry, Maskell, Jones, Truemen, Laver, Sedgman, Mottram, Court, Drobney, and many others. A long list. Frinton's facilities and visiting players ensured that two girls from the Town were good enough to become part of the Whiteman cup team. Miss. Eileen Bennett and Miss. E. Harvey.

It was Viscount Horncastle that had started this Tennis Event. In 1902, when trying to create something special for the Coronation of Edward VII, it was suggested a Tournement might be appealing. This first event only took two weeks from it's conception to it actually taking place, but it was also to be the very first 'International' for the main event was won by New Zealand Champion, C E Hunter who had come to Britain with four other

110

players, to play Wimbledon. All five NZ players played in the first event at Frinton. The ladies winner that year was Miss E.E. Mills. When the club had opened there were only four courts, but by 1926, there were over twenty grass courts, four hard courts and at least 900 members.

From 1919 this event was to take place always for five days, a week or two before Wimbledon. At other times they held special events, or invited personalities to play, and as such in the 1920's the British Ladies Team, which included Mrs Godfrey, came to play a Ladies team from Frinton.

It was really the efforts of one man that ensured the Frinton Tennis Club remained continually vibrant in the earlier days. From 1914 until 1933 the backbone of the club was Percy 'Popsey' Bangs, the secretary, who realized the requirements to sustain a 'great' club, and evolved the things that take place today regarding Tennis events. Sadly owing to the monies now demanded by players, many are now seen only when they are just starting out, or more often, leading senior players attend with their 'sale by date' having gone.

In Walton, Athletics were popular, including a yearly road race from Clacton to Walton. Mixed Hockey. Fishing in the Backwaters and in the Sea. Competitive Cycling, as the Bicycle became more popular. In the Hotels were both Billiards and Snooker with Challenge Shields and Cups. Darts also had leagues before the first world war. The YMCA, or as it is known in Walton, the Red Triangle, was originally a wooden hut, built for the Troops stationed in Walton in the 1914/1918 period. They started Table Tennis at the beginning of it's popularity in the 1920's, and they also had Gymnastics and Physical Training. Badminton was being played both indoors and outdoors. Boxing. Sword and Sabre Fighting. Various forms of Wrestling. On one occasion the great Japanese exponent, and World Middle Weight Wrestling Champion, Mr. Yukio Tani, came to the Pavilion on the Pier in the early 1920's and took on all comers in wrestling, against boxers and even street fighters, using his Jui-Jutsu skills. Peter Chumbley continues this tradition with his Judo Club at the Red Triangle seventy years later.

In 1978, at the Martello Holiday Camp the biggest Skateboard Park in Britain, and some considered it possibly the largest in Europe, was to be

111

built but, owing to the popularity of this 'sport' having diminished by the time it opened, after two years they decided to cut their financial losses, and simply filled the site in, and had it turfed over.

As indicated, few top liners in the entertainment world ever professionally performed in Walton or Frinton when they were at their peak. Pierrot shows that travelled the East Coast, came to Walton regularly. Black Faced minstrels would walk through the town, singing and strumming Banjos. The Hurdy Gurdy man and occasionaly a man with a dancing bear. Punch and Judy was known over a hundred and fifty years ago in Walton, and Len Blease today is available not only to recreate a Mr. Punch that can no longer beat his wife, but he will also provide an evening of Magic when requested. Jack Watlings Summer Theatre in Frinton each year struggles on, and always with threatened closure through lack of finances, and yet there are a host of leading actors today who found their first Theatrical triumphs in Frintons Summer Theatre which has been held at the W.I. Hall in Frinton for many years.

A tendency to stick heads under the shifting sands in recent years, has remained paramount in Frinton. In the late 1920's the Imperial Hall had been built in Pole Barn Lane by local builder Thomas Moy. A Theatre, Cinema, and a place for Dances which became one of the leading centres within the area. The war brought about change and after it was over, the building was to be used (as it is today) as a furniture repository. Even in 1985 the original Stage and projection booth were still in place.

The community was twice offered this building. Firstly when there was talk of a Community Centre. The Imperial and the Seaman's Dairy building, which was also in Pole Barn Lane, were linked as a package to create the Frinton Community Centre. The potential for this dual site were great and should have been grabbed with both hands, but the story of this fiasco needs the letters pages in the local press to tell the fuller story as to what happened, and why the Frinton Community Centre is now at the Triangle (which is not even in Frinton) and using an inappropriate empty Supermarket building which is too difficult for many elderly living within Frinton itself to get to, and it has cost a large and continuing amount of money to alter and at least three times that which the two buildings in Pole

112

Barn Lane could have been obtained for. Even, an alternative proposal, of a 'new built to specifications building' on a site available and designated for a Community Centre some years earlier, could have been used, and a place built for a fifth of the amount gathered and of that spent todate.

Then in the 1980's, the owner of the Imperial Hall stated that, as it hadn't been sold as part of the Community Centre, he still wished the Hall to return to it's correct and proper usage and wished the community to have it. He then asked a price that was ridiculously low. It was an amount never announced publically, as he didn't even tell his family how low the figure was, to ensure there would be no stoppages regarding it going through, but there were those living close to the building, who created lies, myths and stories, to ensure the sale did not happen.

One of the myths they proclaimed was the lack of parking facilities for a building that could seat no more that 350 people, and yet within a short distance there were 'legitimate' parking places (that is places simply not utalising spaces in front of houses) for over 1000 Car parking spaces within the Gates. It was also pointed out that there was an Ambulance Station and a Police Station in Pole Barn Lane. Six years later the Police had gone. Now it has to go to the very top, the Ministry, before it can ever revert to it's original glory and usage as a Theatre and Cinema.

It has a fine fully sprung Maple Wood floor (possibly one of the best in Anglia), which was used in earlier times for Tea Dances and Functions, and as such, the building was 'perfect'. Yet the strange considerations and attitudes of a few narrow minded people, ruined the potential pleasure of thousands, and the financial gains that would have done so much to invigorate the community of Frinton.

As a footnote to this unhappy saga, the local papers provide some part of the story. They show the ludicrous attitudes of a few people living within Frinton. A leading member of the 'Friends of the Frinton Summer Theatre' stood up in the local Council and stated that whilst she remembered the Hall with great affection, she suggested that it should become a Museum, but definitely not a Theatre!!

A Committee was urgently set up to try and 'Save the Imperial', yet strangely, the one person who created difficulties was the representative

113

of the 'Friends of Frinton Theatre', who also did everything to stop it becoming a Theatre again, with arguments at all stages.

Jack Watling was shown the 'Hall' and he stated that it must be reopened, and not just for 'his' Summer Theatre, but for Youth Theatre, Cinema, Tea Dances, other Theatrical groups, as well as Classical Music Concerts. Far too late the main objector in Council, as well as the representative of the 'Friends' on the 'Save the Imperial Committee', decided to change their minds and their objections. Accordingly, there is now a Leisure Centre in Walton which will probably take over the role of the 'Frinton Summer Theatre' at some time in the future. It will have to, and then the name will change to become the 'Walton and Frinton Summer Theatre' and so it will ensure another aspect of bringing greater deprivation to the shops and the area of Frinton accordingly.

As indicated one of the major statements for the Imperial not being accepted was one of parking, yet within ten minutes walk of the Imperial Hall there were/are over 1000 legitimate parking places within the Gates (over 250 within five minutes), which would have disturbed few, and this was a for a 350 seater purpose built building. It was another example of the few not wanting anything that may bring people into Frinton, and something that would have assisted and helped boost the continual flagging prosperity that the Town has suffered for the last forty years.

A very small Museum of local History can be found at the old Railwaymans Cottage by the Gates at Frinton, but it is only opened Tuesday mornings, even throughout the Summer months. Another Museum resides at the old Lifeboat House in Walton, but although obtained for usage as a Museum showing 'Local History' it suddenly changed without any notification to become a Maritime Museum, and even that has widened with Exhibitions which have nothing to do with the area it is suppossed to represent.

In the late 1980's 'The Wick' became vacant when the Council changed it's offices to a site at the Triangle. It was suggested that this building should become the 'Tendring Museum'. This was a factor that would have ensured a steady stream, of what Frintonians would have classified, as the 'right people' and which would have been a small way to assist the economy in the shops locally.

114

Instead the Library Services took it over and yet, as the upper floors were vacant, it was again suggested that these rooms at least take over the role of the Area Museum, but, with the greed of man, and although the building was truthfully the communities, the top of the building was changed and altered into flats, which were sold privately, ensuring that the building can never revert to it's former self.

This is all just another aspect of the lack of understanding regarding the needs locally. Throughout the Tendring Hundreds there are many fragmented collections of varying sizes and put together by interested individuals, some of which overlap and still, in 1993 Tendring has no central Museum.

Had The Wick been utalised as a Museum, the author of this book, in a weak moment, publically stated he was willing to supply over 2000 photographs of local interest from his own extensive collection, and which would have cost him twice as many pounds to produce. 'The Wick' is a vital loss to the Community, even if it now houses a Library.

Chapter 11   THE LIFEBOAT AND HEROISM

By the mid-1750's, Walton was classified as a fishing village and within the community there have always been those who have been willing to brave the waters. To row or sail in even the most dangerous conditions in an attempt to rescue others. or salvage shipping.

It was indicated that a Lifeboat station was needed and the vicar of Walton, the Rev. R J Cooke, suggested that only a small amount of money would be needed. It was some months later being stated that a Boat could not become a reality because of the additional high costs needed to build a proper Lifeboat House. The Local paper three years later declared the reason there could be no RNLI Lifeboat was that there was no suitable place to launch it, although by that time, a large sum of money had been gathered and there was beginning to be an apathy by local residents towards the Lifeboat fund, which they were giving to and seeing nothing in return.

It is known that George Polley had been using his own Boat as a Lifeboat and then, with fund raising he decided to jump the gun, and in September showed off the 'Excelsior' Voluntary Lifeboat at the Waterman's Regatta for the first time. Six months later the boat had some major problems on a pleasure trip around the Lightship, and it had to have extensive repairs. The crew used a Barn besides the Bath House Hotel.

Voluntary Boats in earlier times had created a bad name in rescue work, for they were known as 'scavangers', and were often more interested in the cargo than the lives of those on board a sinking ship. Throughout these years and along this Coastline, there were a number of people who were known for chasing wrecks. This situation throughout the Country had became rife and Parliment stepped in and announced the setting up of the RNLI (Royal Naval Lifeboat Institute), where the saving of lives was paramount.

In 1881 a newspaper stated that E Alfred Arnold had given a large sum of money towards the Walton Lifeboat, and yet the RNLI when asked, indicate they have no record of this. Presumably this also had been given locally and all the gathered funds, from residents and visitors alike, had been banked awaiting a decision.

Because RNLI Boats were not cheap, Voluntary Boats in many areas continued to have a presence, but slowly as more RNLI Boats were to be launched, the independant Boats decreased in number, and where Walton was concerned, it was the Hon. Artillery Company and their Dramatic Club deciding in 1879 that they would like to sponsor a Boat, that was to produce the one to be launched in Walton.

It has always been suggested that the Boat was selected to be housed at Walton because of the Hon. Artillery's links with the Town. Yet as they had not visited nor camped at Walton since the 1850's, this reason is doubtful. It has been also put forward that one of the Sgt. Majors in the Dramatic Club had a link (maybe he met his wife when at one of the camps) but what ever it was, and why, is now lost in time, but their 'link' was purely that it was the RNLI who selected Walton as a base because a boat was definitely needed there and, as the Hon. Artillery Company provided the full amount of money, their name was given to it. The Lifeboat House was built and equipped by RNLI funds and not, as again has always been stated, provided by further money from the Hon Artillery. The building costing £487. 10s plus a further £57. 10s for a roadway onto the beach.

116

To gather the funds the Hon. Artillery Company Dramatic Company put on Theatrical performances, as well as other events. For the Officers, 'Smoking Concerts' were arranged, and talk of Dan Leno attending at least one of these is suggested, but this could be a figment of someones imagination, as no record of his appearance has yet been established, although the Colonel in Chief of the Regiment, Prince Edward (who became King Edward Vll), did attend some of these events.

Five years later, on the 18th Nov.1884, a magnificent Boat having cost £394. 10s and made in Limehouse, by Forrest and Son, was ready. The Lifeboat House was completed on land provided by Robert Warner at a nominal rent. The Duke of Portland was the Lt. Colonel of the Regiment, and his wife Lady Bolsover officially launched the Boat. The Regimental Band and 150 members of the Hon. Artillery were in attendance. The town was bedecked in flags and it was a public Holiday. Coastguards from Harwich, Clacton and Walton, as well as the The Warner Foundry Band were on parade with the County Constabulary and the Clacton Lifeboat towed in procession by six horses. This boat had already saved ninety six lives during it's short seven years in existance.

Lady Bolsover stated 'I name this boat The Honourable Artillery Company and I hope and trust and pray that, manned by it's Storm Warriors, it may always be succesful in saving human lives'. She then broke a bottle of wine on the side of the boat, and it was launched by the crew. The Boat was 37 feet long and nine foot wide and could self right itself if it capsized, within 35 seconds.

That night, between 11.00 and mid-night, a signal was seen from the Sunk Lightship and the Lifeboat was again launched, but on a rescue for the very first time. It was unsuccesful, as they could not find any boat, and they returned to base by 7. 00 the next morning. Over the following weeks they were to go out a number of times and in December 1884, they saved 25 men from the ship 'Deike Rickers' of Bremenhaven in Germany, which ended up on Long Sand. It was here that the illustrious future of the Walton RNLI Boats began.

The launcher they had, based on the distance from the sea to the Lifeboat House, was a carriage or frame in which the Boat rested and large thin wooden wheels to tow it to the water. The sands, and the distance that the

117

Sea goes out along this Coastline, ensured that the men had at times to struggle to launch it, especially at low tide. Up to two and a half hours! Apparently no launch was less than half an hour in length, although until the end of it's life, in 1900, the boat was involved in saving a total of 132 lives.

It was because of the launching problems that eventually lifeboats were to be left moored in the sea, and the men taking smaller craft to row to the main boat. Now they utalise the Pier, and, after changing in the new Lifeboat House they run, grab bicycles and pedal along the pier to where they go down steps to a small boat, which takes them to the Lifeboat. Now it can take only a very short amount of time from the call coming through, to starting the motors and getting under way

Between 1884 and the present time there have been six main Boats, starting with the Hon. Artillery (1884 to 1900); The James Stevens No. 14 (1900 to 1928); E. M. E. D. (1928 to 1953); The Edian Courtald (1953 to 1977); Earl and Countess Howe (1977 to 1983); City of Birmingham (1984 until the end of 1993) plus a number of Temporary Boats which take over when the Walton Boats are in for repair or overhaul. In addition there have been four 'Boarding Boats' which became established from 1900 onwards.

Two questions often asked: What do the EMED initials stand for and why is the John Stephens numbered No. 14?

Firstly regarding the E.M.E.D: There were four people that put up money for a Boat and each asked for a relatives name to be used. This Boat was 48 and a half foot long and 13 foot wide. The EMED was officially launched in July 1930 by Prince George when he opened Princes Esplanade in the Town, although it had been at Walton nearly two years on rescue work. None of the people that had asked for their choice of name for the Boat had provided enough finances individually, and so, as this was a joint financial effort, it was decided to link all the names together, by using the Christian names of the four that had been put forward: Ellen (Dewhurst); Mortimer (Yates); Eliza (Baines) and Dudley (Watkins): E.M.E.D.

The second query is why the 'James Stevens' is numbered No.14. The reason here is that the benifacter gave in total 21 boats to the RNLI, and Walton's was No. 14. It was a boat 43 foot long, and 12 and a half foot wide, and assisted in saving a total of 227 lives.

During the last one hundred and ten years, Walton's Lifeboats have saved

118

a total of over 8OO people on major rescues.

RNLI Boats have always had a problem whereby they are not allowed to go out on a rescue unless they have been summoned to do so. This was understandable, for in the early days, a boat could go looking and in the time before Radio Communication, based on wrong information, and in a large expanse of water, in very rough seas, a Ship in trouble, with men (and sometimes women) needing to be saved, could easilly be missed, owing to them looking in the wrong direction.

The Iron Lighthouse (185O) which had an eleven mile range of light, and which stood at Gunfleet Sands, eventually had one of the earliest telephone cable links, laid from Frinton, for they were in a better position to see into the distance than those on land. The Sunk Lightship had a telegraphic line in 1882. The top of the Trinity House Landmark on the Naze was also used for visual sightings

Yet, in poor weather, seldom can a long distance be seen. The Voluntary Boats could go looking. Both those in Walton over twenty three years (188O/1884 and 1894/1911), and that in Frinton, for sixteen years (19O1/1917), were willing to risk their lives, often rowing much of the time when sail could not be used, looking for a possible wreck.

Normally in the days way before Radio and distress rockets, a crew member from a damaged ship had to get off his boat, and try and get to the shore. Then run or generally stagger to someone with a horse (in the days before the telephone), and get to the Lifeboat House. A signal would be sounded to gather the crew together. The delay in launch, especially the first Boat, and then en-route to where the wreck was known to have been, could have meant hours lost, whereas the Voluntary, looking and seeking, managed to find boats in trouble, although there were many occasions when they went out and found nothing, after being on dangerous seas for hours.

In Walton the 'Excelsior' Lifeboat (188O/84) was followed by a second private Boat 'True to the Core' in 1894, after there was a private argument between Polley and Crew members of the RNLI. It was to be like most Voluntary Boats, and doubled as a Pleasure Boat during the Summer season, taking visitors to see the Light Ship or in those earlier days, the Light House. There is now no indication as to what happened regarding all of the various monies that had been gathered in Walton for a Boat, it is

119

presumed that this was utalised by G. Polley for his 'own' private Lifeboat, or for the first 'True to the Core', or the second, which was to follow, and which again was named 'True to the Core'.

David Cook, a fisherman who had been a member of the Lowerstoft Lifeboat crew, moved to Frinton, and initially for a few months used his own Boat to act as a Lifeboat, but in 1901 he raised £12. OO to buy the 'Godsend', which had been Lowerstofts original Boat on which he had served. This had been sold when the RNLI acquired a new boat there. Fortunately for Frinton, the fisherman who purchased it, was a friend of Cooks, and was willing to make a profit of £8. OO, having bought it originally from the RNLI for only £4. OO.

Cook renamed the Boat the 'Sailors Friend', and then in 1907 made arrangements to have a slightly bigger Boat built in Harwich, which again was called the 'Sailors Friend'. When this was launched at Harwich, the bottle smashed over the hull, was not a rare wine, but a bottle of Sea Water, as all the men on that Lifeboat were, and remained, Teetotalers

The Great War in 1914 ensured that men left to fight for their country, and crew members of the Voluntary Boats took the places of the RNLI Crew who enlisted or were called up. After the war finished, neither Voluntary boat was restarted. There had been prior to the War a number of occasions when both the Walton Voluntary or the Frinton Boat were to assist the RNLI Boat. In some cases the RNLI Boat arrived first, and then on other occasions they were to pull alongside after one of the Voluntary Boats had been in attendance. There was though a continual problem, whereby, RNLI crewmen disliked the Voluntary crews, and this created an 'us and them' attitude in some of the homes where brothers were to be members of both lifeboats.

With the end of the Second War and the introduction of radar navigation and electronic communications, nearly everything needed by the Lifeboats or Helicopters is available, although the actual human factor is still as important as it ever was, when seas are bad and men are giving their lives for others. There are still a few Voluntary Boats throughout the country, but generally only within areas where no RNLI Boats are readily available, and, unlike the pre-1914 War period, today the RNLI work closely with these

120

Boats and what they do.

The RNLI Crew have been involved in many major rescues, but only a few have remained in the memory, with possibly in recent years that of Radio Caroline in 1966 and the publicity it created that will always link it's name with the Walton Boat.

The E.M.E.D. in May 1940, was taken out of the crews hands, when Dunkirk was being evacuated, and the military put their own men on board. The Officer in charge of the Boat was killed during that action.

The RNLI Boats in Walton represents over 100 years of heroism

Devotion to saving lives, as oppossed to crew members normal work has always been primary. An example of this was shown when the signal went up and Billy Hall, one of the Frinton Postmen, was delivering the mail. He stopped the first person in the street, and gave them his bag and all the letters, and asked the passerby to deliver them to the Post Office at the bottom of Connaught Avenue, as it was not en-route to the Lifeboat. Unfortunately a fog came down whilst they were out and it was three days before he managed to report back to work. This was a serious deriliction of duty, and he was brought before a Post Office Tribunal. When asked to explain himself, Hall stated that he felt peoples lives were more important than His Majesties Mails. This was apparently accepted, and as nothing was missing, he was exonerated.

Anyone that risk their lives for others are heroes, be they the RNLI crew now, or the various crews of the past. Neither RNLI members, or those that were on the Voluntary Boats, would classify themselves as being anything more than ordinary, yet the RNLI Crewmen in Walton have been awarded nine Bronze medals and four Silver and Frinton Voluntary Lifeboatman David Cook, who took people for trips on his Boat, and had Bathing Machines on Frinton Sands, was involved in saving in excess of 1000 lives, indicating the peril that some have been in, and this must always be remembered.

Other acts of herosim, are seldom remembered and it often needs the jogging of peoples memories for them to re-emerge. This happened when the Bronze bust of H.G. Columbine was stolen in Walton in 1990. Only a few locally knew his name, or why a bust had been erected. Yet he gave his life and had been awarded the Victoria Cross for his bravery during the first

World War.

As the years progress there are people who are unaware why there is a memorial stone on 'The Leas', to Brian Bishop, at the end of Central Avenue. There have been and are other heroes, but these are generally not known to the majority, having reached this distinction prior to their arriving within the community.

One like this was J Norwood, a member of Frinton Golf Club who was to lose his life within a few days of the outbreak of the first world war. The list of club members who gave their lives during that War can be seen on the left as you enter the clubhouse, and Norwoods name stands out, because it shows he was a Victoria Cross holder.

Norwood had been a second Lieutenant with the 5th Dragoon Guards. On mounted Patrol, he found his Troop were in the middle of a group of snipers and one of his men was hit. Norwood returned to the man, and whilst continuosly under heavy fire, dismounted, picked the man up and carried him on his shoulders, whilst leading his horse with his other hand. When they were out of range of fire, he eased the man to the ground, ensured he was alright, until a medical team could pick him up, and remounting, he rejoined his Troop. This was during the Boer War and within a few days the problems of Ladysmith had started. The date was 30th October 1899 and for his outstanding bravery, in assisting another whilst under fire, he was awarded the V.C.

He was like many ex-Military living in Frinton, a member of the Frinton Rifle Club, who used the ranges on the Naze, and like 30 others of that same club, he and they, were all to sign up immediately there was a hint of war, with many reporting back to their original Regiments. Norwood was a reservist and was to be attached again to the 5th Dragoons with the rank of Captain, and, like so many within those sad early days when, as throughout the four years, a great loss of life happened, he was to die in action on the 8th September 1914, just a few days after war had officially been declared.

Private Columbine on the other hand was not to lose his life until 22nd March 1918, for 'most conspicious bravery and Self Sacrifice'. Owing to many casualities, he took command of a gun post, which he and two others held for four hours. When aeriel bombing took place, and when he saw the enemy gaining ground on both sides, he ordered those with him to escape

122

whilst he covered their retreat. He then remained and inflicted continual and tremendous losses to the enemy. He was eventually killed by a bomb explosion hitting where he was positioned.

Two months later it was announced that he had been posthumously awarded the Victoria Cross. The Medal was passed to the Town by his mother, and the custody of it had been passed to the British Legion, although the Town still has ownership. A bust of Columbine was made and unveiled on the 21st Nov. 1920, and stood for many years on the Marine Gardens, but this was changed to a site by Walton Church. After it had been stolen in 1990, a replica was made, and then the original turned up, and it is now in the Leisure Centre, which bears his name. A replica of the medal can now be seen at the Old Lifeboat House.

On the 22nd August 1984, Colin Richards, aged 35, entered Walton Post Office with a sawn off Shotgun and demanded money. He filled his holdall, and got onto a Motor Bike, and went straight to Frinton Post Office and held them up, but with an alarm going he fled empty handed from Frinton, and drove off in the direction of Central Avenue.

As he crossed over the bridge, he threw his holdall into the bushes at the side of the road. A lady walking her dog saw this, and went to examine it and found it contained £8705 pounds. She called the Police. They set up a watch, with eight armed Police.

At approx. Eight Thirty that evening, a figure went directly to the bag and picked it up. 37 year old PC Brian Bishop, who was within the team, an acting sergeant and 39 yr old Det. Sgt Mervyn Farnworth, stood up and cautioned the man. The outcome was Colin Richards shot them both, hitting Farnworth in the groin, but hitting Bishop in the head. Another Policeman stood and cautioned, but before Richards could fire again, he was shot by the police.

All three were rushed to hospital, where surgery ensured Farnsworth was released within a few days. Bishop who had come from Chelmsford, was taken to London in a desperate bid to save his life, but he never recovered and died five days later.

Colin Richards at the time of his Trial at Norwich Crown Court, was paralysed and in a wheel chair, and whilst he denied murder, there was no sympathy for his condition based on what he had done, for he received what amounted to a life sentence

As the years progress, heroism in any form, will be queried by each growing generation, and there will always be those who suggest that such acts are foolhardy, and with time and attitudes always changing, some of the great historical figures whose deeds are known, will be looked at with little understanding by modern eyes or appreciation of the age in which they happened.

Yet everyone does what he feels is right 'at the time'. How many people who have acted in a spontaneous way, to save a life (or lives), when asked, can truthfully give an honest answer as to why they did what they did.

Chapter 12   MODERN TIMES and Entertainment

The changes that have taken place in Walton, and the build-up of Frinton, can be seen visually. Kirby and Great Hollands growth was to be of a stop and start nature, with a general slowing down regarding building work within the early part of the 1800's and then, after a lull, there was a slight surge within Kirby Cross when the Railways arrived. It was in the 1950/60's that a major growth started in both Frinton and Walton, when it was realized that it had become too expensive to buy similar properties on the South Coast.

In 1900 Amateur entertainment in Walton was held at the Public Hall or at the Saville Hall in Saville Street and in the same year a Town Hall costing £8000 was built, wherein there was the 'Kings Theatre' and here varied entertainments, both professional and amateur took place. This building was closed in 1934, sold and pulled down. 'The Albion' was extended at the rear of the Hotel and provided a place of entertainment seating 400 people in 1908.

On the Pier in the 1900's, they had not only 'The Pavilion' where stage shows were presented, but also by 1910, there was the 'Sea Spray', a building at the front of the Pier, which had Tea Dances and more genteel entertainment. Here the Sea Spray Orchestra or the Kai-Ora Dance Band, Dexters Band or Red Smiths Orchestra played throughout the season.

On the beach a wooden stage stood for many years where the Pierrots, such as Catlins Royal Pierrots or Victor and Vestas Party Pierrots would give their performances. On the Pier there were Roundabouts and early slot machines, showing Ghost Houses and laughing Clowns. The earliest form of cinema 'What the Butler Saw', costing one penny, always stopped as it was getting interesting. Gaming laws pre-war ensured that those 'of chance' were illegal, although 'Cranes', to hopefully pick up a packet of cigarettes (they were often five Woodbines) or a small bar of chocolate, were acceptable, as were pinballs into slots, providing a possible winner, for these were classified as games of 'skill', ensuring they got around the laws on gambling at that time.

By 1920 in Frinton, there were over 220 residental homes and 150 commercial establisments (shops, Hotels, etc). Silent Cinema performances were regularly being held two or three times a week at 'Victors', or as it became, the 'Queens Hall' in Connaught Avenue. This had been built in 1918 for dances and stage shows but cinema was found most popular, and by 1925 during some weeks, peformances were held every day, excluding Sunday, where during these years no place of entertainment or shop ever opened on the Sabbath.

In Walton it was the 'Kino' that brought cinema to the people, but in 1934 the 'Regal' opened in Waltons High Street. This even offered an opportunity for Tea and sandwiches in elegant surrounds, prior to seeing a 'Talkie'. The 'Kino' had originally been silent, and it wasn't until two or three years after sound came, that it also had made the change.

The 'Regal' opened on the 5th May 1934 with a private showing of the 'Blue Mountain', a German Film, and then two days later, on the 7th of May, they officially opened with Myrna Loy and William Powell in 'Every Woman's Man'. The owner Victor Harrison had high hopes of the Cinema doing well. He bought the 'Kino' as well, but then sold the Walton Cinema's to the Ager Chain. During the war the Army took them over for lectures and their own training films. The 'Regal' was then handed back in early 1941 to keep up the moral of the locals remaining in the Town, with a good dose of George Formby, Will Hay and Gracie Fields films.

In Kirby, entertainment took place in the Church Hall, including Lantern Slide shows. In the 20's and 30's silent cinema, and later, a few sound films were shown occasionaly on 9.5 mm, but these were not regular

125

events. In 1909 Great Holland built their small Village Hall, then just prior to the 1st World War they installed a Bath House where on a Friday night it cost 6d a Bath (children 3d) using tokens purchased from the Post Office. Memorial Halls were to be built in the 1920's, and a British Legion Hall was built in Walton in 1931.

In Frinton, in the late-1920's, the Queens Cinema was to close once the Imperial Hall had been built and was showing films. Unlike the 'Queens', the Imperial wasn't used solely as a cinema, as the first week it was hired at a cost of £25 by Stanley Holloway and his Troupe, but once a projection booth and sound system had been installed in the 1930's it was to show films fairly regularly.

In Walton in 1930, after the Bowls Green had been moved from the Round Gardens, it was to be filled with Childrens Roundabouts and a Carousel, but this was to be changed after four years and a Wood and Glass building was erected. A Night Club named the Road House opened it's doors during 1934. It was announced that a Cabaret would take place nightly and Meals and drinks could be purchased. During the day parties of trippers used the Dining Rooms. A small open air swimming pool was also opened alongside it. Within eight months the club closed and the swimming pool was altered to become a Lily Pond. The building within a year was taken down as nobody wanted it, and the Lily pond was removed as children were using it to paddle in, and the Round Gardens became as they are now.

When the war started, both Frinton and Walton were empty of visitors as they were restricted areas. Home owners were allowed to remain or those living elsewhere, could visit to check the properties they owned against any damage caused through bombing, otherwise officially nobody was allowed into the area. As war progressed, and things became easier, a small number of foreign V.I.P's were allowed to live in Frinton for short periods. The Beaches from the Naze to Jaywick were thick with barbed wire. Mines had been laid, and Pill Boxes erected. The Pier had two holes blown in it. In Frinton the Beach Hotel was destroyed in 1941 when a bomb fell directly into one of the chimneys and exploded within the building. The saddest result of this was over 80 years of glass negatives taken by J.A.Jones, the local photographer, were destroyed. They showed the growth of Frinton and Walton, and had been stored at the Beach Hotel once war had started.

126

As war ended and peace settled, the two seaside Towns slowly tried to regain what they had before the War. The Tennis Week in Frinton was restarted. For twenty five years, it continued to bring the leading players, but finances made it impossible once the game became open and money was the order of the day. Golf did not manage to draw the same pre-war big names, because there was no Royalty to attract them. In fact the only entertainment in Frinton of note was the continuing subsidence or as happened in 1964, when thousands of tons of earth and mud actually slid over the tops of the beach huts and into the Sea. This brought in the crowds.

In 1883 there had a been a complaint that Walton had no Fire Engine. Soon after this, one was obtained and it was housed at the Porto Bello Family Hotel Stables. It was then re-housed in a building in Saville Street, with the Horse Drawn Fire Engine in 1913 being called the 'Welcome'. In Frinton a Fire Engine became a reality at the turn of the century. It was housed by The Wick prior to it getting a Station in Pole Barn Lane. It was for a time nicknamed the 'Baker Boys Wagon', when Charlie and Frank, the two sons of Moon, the Bakers in Old Road, were members of the crew.

The need for a Fire Engine was shown in the mid-1930's when Mummery's, a large store in Connaught Avenue caught fire and burnt down. A lad working in the Council Offices named Brian Sparling saw the blaze and ran to the Fire Station and sounded the alarm. As it became worse, the Engine from Walton was called out to assist.

With the exception of the Fire Chief, all the crew members were Voluntary. In Kirby and Gt. Holland they relied upon bucket chains, which had been a problem in the years before running water was freely available. From 1908, a yearly competition was held on the Greensward in Frinton to show off the local Firemens skills with their style and efficiency. Ladder climbing and saving life. A Challenge Shield was on offer and teams started to come from Clacton and Harwich and other local towns, although it was rumoured that 'other' teams stopped coming when, during one years competition, a house had burnt down because the engine was at Frinton.

Whilst many towns had Police Constables, there was only one Policeman within Walton during the 1870's, although each year, and especially during the holiday period, the number of visitors grew far more than one man could handle and P.C. Tuffin stated (as did the town council)

127

that more Police were needed. Six Parish Constables were then sworn in. In 1881 P.C. Jason Blatt joined Tuffin, and he was followed by a Sergeant and another full time Constable four months later, and during August Bank Holiday of that year, 10 additional Specials and Police were brought in from other areas because of the large crowds visiting the town.

For years Walton kept requesting that they have a 'lock up', to hold prisoners, and the Board in Chelmsford kept refusing, indicating it was not necessary. Kirby had a Police Constable (PC 170) as early as 1857, but from the 1880's, those stationed in Walton were called out if anything serious happened in either Frinton, Great Holland or Kirby. With the growth of Frinton, and the 'rich' who were living there, by 1910 they had two men on duty throughout most of the year in Old Road, and once Royalty put in appearance in the 1920's, this number was increased during the season (Easter to October). They were eventually to move the Police Station to a house in Pole Barn Lane (now closed).

By 1904 the telephone was becoming available. It cost £3.00 yearly and for a further 30/- each year you could make as many local calls as you wished. This today sounds generous, except that at the time there were in that year only seventeen phones in the whole of Frinton, and less in Walton, and only three or four in Kirby, and Gt. Holland.

Although the Churches had their own cemetaries a general one was needed, and a site in Kirby was selected in 1918. The locals protested that 'continual funeral processions would effect the value of houses along the route' to which one of the council said that 'six each year might just do this!!'

As time progressed, there were to be many changes. New properties were built. Houses taken down and blocks of flats put up in their place. Large old houses changed to become flats or in recent years, old peoples homes. The Naze has continually crumbled away.

The Marine Hotel, in Walton, became known as Barkers Hotel. The owner at that time was an eccentric. He would not allow crisps to be sold in his bar, because they 'were too noisy'.

In Walton, the land the two Mills had been sited on, was taken over by the Yacht Club in 1922, after one of the mills had fallen down and the other had been removed. The Yacht Club had originally run their affairs from a

128

small shack in Mill Lane and in 1910 they had found a suitable place for administration above some shops in the High Street. 'Halls' the Boat Builders have remained in Walton building and repairing boats for nearly a hundred years. In Frinton, the Ironmongers, Blowers and Coopers have been in evidence ninety years and still going strong. They started business in Old Road in 1903 and then in 1912 moved to the shop next door to where they are today. The Porto Bello Hotel in Walton is now a mixture of shops, and both the Frinton Lodge and Grand Hotels have become Retirement Residential Flats.

Continually people came to the area, however big the attraction of Clacton or other seaside resorts. August Bank Holiday in 1930 brought in over 2500 Excursion Rail ticket holders to Walton. A further 300 were purchased to go to Frinton.

Cheering could be heard throughout the district when the British R101 Airship flew over, and four years later, in 1934, the German 'Graf Zeppelin' was seen slowly flying past. On the ground, that same year, a central refuse tip was being proposed for Kirby. It was rejected by every adult living in Kirby Cross and Kirby Le Soken (over 800). It didn't make any difference to the Council, and some years later the tip was to be opened.

From the early 1900's there were yearly gatherings to see Baptisms at Sea which took place prior to the Gospel Mission and the Free Churches getting their own Baptismal Pools. In 1912, C.S.S.M. (The Christian Spiritual Scripture Mission) started their yearly gathering for Children who came to Frinton for a week (or two weeks) get together. There had been for a few years, between the wars, a similar week held in Walton as well. After exactly 80 years, the organisation changed, and these weeks are now organised by a number of local Churches. Tom Rees, an evangalist purchased the Esplanade Hotel in Frinton and created a Christian meeting place during the 1930's, renaming the Hotel, 'Hillingborough Hall'.

During the Post War years in Walton, the Pier tried to gain more customers by having many different Entertainments, including a Ten Pin Bowling Alley (1964). There was a Ferris Wheel, but this was to be removed after a number of gale force winds indicated the Pier might collapse through it being there. The stage shows that had been so important pre-war were unable to restart, as the 'Pavilion' had been struck by lightening during

129

the war, and the 'Sea Spray' was burnt down by a cigarette dropped by a soldier in the 1940's. Neither were re-built and now the end of the Pier is used mainly by fishermen.

The fields around the Bath House Meadow in Walton at the turn of the Century had been producing Fruit from the Orchards and a range of Vegetables. It was owned or rented predominently by Mr. Archer the Greengrocer, but this altered and changed with the Bath House Meadow becoming amongst other things a Holiday Caravan Site and a Car Park in recent years. It was used for the entertainments during the Regattas. For local sports meetings. Special Events and even Fun Fairs. From 1967 it was used by the Carnival. It now has a very small Swimming Pool, a Leisure Centre and Indoor Bowling Green, and both await the floods that will happen in a few years time.

Other than Farming, there was never a great amount of Industry locally. The Copperas Works closed. Brick making was important during the growth of the area, but these Works closed when the quantities of bricks needed diminished, and commercial makers took over the needs of modern day builders.

From the 1870's, and for the next fifty years, Warners Foundry provided the largest number of jobs in Walton. The Railways needed people at the sidings in Kirby, Walton and at Frinton, not only to offload but also to deliver the goods as well. There were fishermen. In Frinton there was Henry Ratcliffes, who owned the first garage in the Town. They hired out Bathchairs. They made, as well as supplied for rent or purchase, Bicycles. They even made an early Motor Cycle as well, and in Gt. Holland they owned the East Essex Ironworks, opposite the Village Hall, where, from 1888 they produced Plough shares and Drain Covers, but then after a period when it was not used, from 1919 they developed Farming Equipment and were to produce a popular Garden mower that sold throughout Britain (as well as overseas). This works was to eventually close in 1975.

There was in both Frinton and Walton an Electric works, and Walton had for years a Water Works, which ceased once water was piped from Mistley. It also had a Gas Works, and from 1900 there has been little else, for it was the Holiday Industry that sustained Walton and Frinton. Farming provided the earnings for the majority in both Kirby and Gt. Holland.

130

So it remained until all four towns became the haven of the 'commuter' and a retirement centre, and in Frintons case, from the early 1980's, over 60 percent living in the Town are now of pensionable age.

One aspect that has been a problem for people living in Frinton is the element of fun created by it's 'exclusivness'. Often remarks are made by people who have never visited Frinton, basing their comments on reputation alone. When mentioned in TV sitcoms, the suggestion is that Frinton is the place where only the 'rich' or the 'snobs' reside and it was often joked that 'Lord Snooty' in the Beano must have had a place there, and more recently, in the cartoon strip, which appears in both National and London papers, 'Bristow' has an Auntie Maude living in Frinton. Yet the town is nothing like this, and is now definitely up to date, whereby, unless anyone objects, Nude or Topless Sun Bathing are not banned!

Frinton is definitely looking forward to the 21st century!

Chapter 13   TIMES OF WAR

There are two local Walton monuments of the past that are linked with earlier wars. Trinity Tower and the Martello Tower.

The Trinity Tower was built on the Naze to be used as a landmark when ships sailed towards Harwich or when they left it, and it is known that Nelson saw it when he left in the 'Medusa' en-route to fight Napolean in 1801, when his boat and others left Harwich. The Tower had been used from 1795 as a semiphore station and at that time the existing roof was strengthened and raised 14 feet, so the signals could be seen and linked with both Harwich and St. Osyths. The top of the building was also altered internally as well, and enabled the signalling station to be used throughout the Napoleonic war.

In 1903 the Admiralty took over the bulding again, at a yearly rent of one shilling, and a new Semiphore link was set up, as well as at that time, erecting a flagpole as well. It was only returned to Trinity House in 1931, and during the second world war it was taken over yet again, and the concave dishes for Radar were set up on the roof. During April 1957 and until July 1958, the U.S. Government took it over as a potential tracking

131

Station.

This part of the country changed in 1800, when it was thought that Napoleon was going to invade Britain. In 1803 it was established that flat bottom boats were being made in Europe to carry troops across the Channel and in fear of a potential attack, a number of the wealthier locals packed their belongings and were ready to run. It was then that a series of Martello Towers were proposed, to defend the Country.

The news about these boats ensured that there were to be encamped nearly three thousand troops within this part of Essex during the period when the Towers were being built and for some period afterwards. In Weeley a large Barracks was erected and along this Coastline a series of large huts were provided to accomodate, in each, an Officer and up to thirty men, plus stables for eight horses, to ensure the complete length of coastline was guarded.

12 Martello Towers were to be built in Essex, of which one was in Gt. Holland, another in Frinton and two in Walton. It was planned they should all have a Battery in front of them (or along side) on which heavy guns would be placed. (see frontis page). Once built, Britain awaited for 'Boney' to attack.

Everyone living in the area was informed that if an invasion happened they must all move as quickly as possible to Kirby. No other instructions appear to have been given, so it is presumed they then had to sit and greet the French as they arrived at Kirby? A group of farmers were instructed that they must drive all the cattle from this part of the country towards the borders of Cambridgeshire, to ensure that the French would have little to eat when they arrived.

Along the Coast each Martello Tower was given an initial, and the one at Holland Marsh (H) stood in the centre of what is now Frinton Golf Course. It was built on land owned by Charles Hicks, who, as a farmer, owned the land in conjunction with the Naval Knights of Windsor. All of the Towers, except that in Gt. Holland had a Battery, but this may have been because the site in Holland was on Marsh Land and it was doubted whether it could support the weight of the heavy guns and the building which contained it.

All the Towers were built between 1809 to 1811. Great Hollands Tower was the first to be sold after the war, in 1819. It was taken down, with the

132

rubble and stones carted to both Kirby and Great Holland to build cottages.

Frinton (Tower I) was built on what is now the Greensward, which was to became known as Battery Point. It was in line with the end of Second Avenue. W. L Shadwell purchased the site in 1820 but he did not remove the Tower until 1822. He left standing two cottages that had been built alongside it.

Walton's two Towers (J and K) were important as they each differed in their design, and linked together by a single road (known today as Marello Road). The larger one (J) erected on Walton Cliffs (see the drawing of the building on the rear of the cover), and in an area behind what is now the Pier Hotel. In 1810 the land had been owned by three people, Arthur Whitmore, David Brown and Thomas Fisher, which they all agreed, as part of national security, they had to sell to the Government.

This Tower (J) stood within a Moat. In 1826 it was discovered that 17 years after it had been built, the land, between the Battery, which lay due East, and the Tower, had eroded 120 feet, and it was under threat. £82 was offered and accepted for the materials that made up the Battery, and by 1829 they were removed. In 1835 the Tower, it's Guardhouse and the land were put up for sale, and bought for £1255, with the stipulation that the Tower would be taken down before the end of that year.

W Raven bought the land, but then had a dispute with J. Warner the following year, over the boundries. The outcome was that the moat was filled in, and it was converted into the road which is now around the Round Gardens. Between the Towers erection and the sale, over three quarters of an acre had gone from the land between it and the sea. Both this Tower and Walton Hall had been used for a period to house French Prisoners from the war with Napoleon.

Tower (K) is still in Walton. Built on the Backwaters on land purchased from Peyter Scaley. During that war it had a 24 Pounder Gun mounted within the Battery and 'where it remained until after 1816'. This Tower is today the feature of the Martello Holiday Caravan Park. Even the Barracks at Weeley, when they were taken down, were to eventually find their way to Walton, as the rubble was bought and then used in the foundations of many of the buildings being built at the time.

In 1797 a Frenchman was actually captured in Gt. Holland, but only because his fishing boat had ran aground

From the end of the Napoleonic War onwards, there were a series of occasional Military manouvres along the coastline from Walton to Clacton, and it was in 1904 when the Duke of Connaught attended with his wife and two daughters, that they all stayed at the Grand Hotel in Frinton, and it was on this occasion that he agreed to give his name to Connaught Avenue.

Between 1820 and the Great War, Britain was involved in two wars. Firstly the Crimean and then the Boer War. During these years, the adage of every soldier carried a Field Marshalls Baton in his knapsack was nearly proven, when one of Walton's sons, born in 1783, joined the 2nd Life Guards as a 2nd Cornet player, and eventually rose to become General Lord Cathcart.

Normally up until this time, few names, unless they reached a level of importance, are remembered, but during both the 1914/1918 and 1939/1945 wars, individuals names are carved into history in most towns, not for what they did, but that they were the men (and women) who lost their lives serving their country and often listed on amalgamated Memorial Stones, for future generations to see.

There have always been people whose foresight has been ahead of it's time. Phillip Brannon in Walton was not just an Architect, but also an Engineer, a Designer and an Inventor.

In 1879 he had produced a small booklet indicating the feasability of the Airship. He showed and described nearly everything that the Germans were to produce thirty five years later. He also showed clearly how they could be used to drop bombs. The British Government took no interest, although the Army and Navy Magazine was to recognise the potentials. Maybe had someone with vision looked towards the future we would have been well ahead of the Germans and their Airship power, both before, during and after the first world war.

In the early part of 1914/15 troops were stationed locally and many were encamped along this coastline ready for possible invasion. In 1915 King George V and Queen Mary came and visited the men in Frinton, Gt. Holland and Clacton. Troops were billeted wherever there was space. In Gt Holland they were sleeping in the Village Hall and the Rectory. Every

134

House had at least one soldier. Ratcliffes in Frinton became a munitions factory

Zepplins flew over during the day as Brannon had foreseen, but at night when they reached Walton and Frinton, the Zepplins used searchlights to follow the Railway lines to London, where they were to drop their bombs. Unexploded Mines turned up on the beaches and eventually many wounded troops were sent to recuperate in both Walton and Frinton.

Not all fighting took place on the battlefront. In Great Holland a private soldier shot his sergeant and then tried to kill himself. It was stated at the time he was jealous of the amount of time the sergeant was having off, and yet there was another more logical rumour that a young lady might have been the reason. All along the Greensward into Walton and alongside the edge of the Naze, Trenches were dug. They were left until well after the war had finished, although they were very dangerous to both visitors and locals alike, for people, when out for an evening stroll, were regularly falling into them.

Nearly every home in the Country was effected by at least one relative being killed or maimed in action. Memorial crosses were set up everywhere, so those who died would always be remembered. In March 1920 Gt. Holland dedicated one of the earliest War Memorials to be built within the County and which was much more useful than most, as it was a drinking fountain. In Kirby their Memorial Cross was placed at 'Cage Corner' (Halstead and Lower Street) but this was removed and re-erected close bye, during road widening.

In Frinton and Walton in 1920, two 'Vimy' Guns were placed as a 'permanent' memory to all those who had lost their lives in the first World War. The one in Frinton was situated in the Jubilee Garden. Eventually it became covered with Ivy. They were both removed at the start of the second world war, as the steel was needed to make modern guns and Shells.

It seems incredulous that in September 1939 children were evacuated to Kirby and Gt. Holland from London 'for safety'. 120 girls from Edmonton High School, aged between 11 and 16 were sent to this area. They were housed in homes and Church and Village Halls, but as there were was not enough rooms available, a number were moved within the restricted area of

135

Frinton, to the Rock Hotel. Sense then took over and they were moved again, en-block, to Wales.

During the second war there were Poles, Canadians, Czechs and other Nationalities stationed here abouts. In 1941 both the Tennis and Golf Clubs were taken over by the Post Office Home Guard. The Tennis Club was used for lectures, and the Golf Club for Field Training. Over three years, thousands of men (and some women), from all over Essex and Suffolk came to train, until the emergency became less, and when, by February 1943, it was felt the Home Guard were not going to be needed, the Clubs were then returned to the community.

During these years some Tennis Courts had been left playable, and just four holes were usable at the Golf Course. On the rest of the Course there were Tank Traps, and Mines. There were even mines around the Flag pole.

Mainly it was the officers stationed locally that were able to play Tennis or Golf, and, during a game at the Tennis Club in 1942, a handful of players were Machine Gunned by a German Aircraft. Both the V.1 and V.2 Flying Bombs flew over two years later, and at least one exploded on the Golf Course (creating a new bunker) and another fell in Elm Tree Avenue.

Suggested Golfing rules were laid down for all Courses in the country, but anyone who acted on them didn't see the joke:

a) Players are asked to collect all bomb and shell splinters to stop them effecting the mowing machines.
b) During gunfire or bombs dropping, players may take cover without a penalty point.
c) Any delayed Bombs must be marked with a red flag, and a white flag also must be placed to show the safe distance.
d) A ball lying in a crater may be lifted and dropped no nearer than the hole without a penelty
e) A ball moved by the enemy action may be replaced as near as possible to where it lay. If lost or destroyed a ball may be dropped not nearer the hole without penalty.
f) A player whose stroke is affected by a similtaneous explosion of a bomb or shell or machine gun fire, may play another ball from the same place. Penalty. One stroke.

136

It was the Military that saved the Frinton Cricket Ground from being dug up and used for cultivation. The grounds had been given to the community on the understanding that at least one match must be played during a specific period each year. A deed of covenent was produced when there was no reason to believe that there would never be a time when such arrangements could not take place. Once the area became restricted, no matches were being played and it was realized that unless one did take place, within a limited period, there could be no Club in the future. The Military Commander was approached and asked if he could help, and through him, they staged a cricket match especially, which ensured that the Club remains as it is today.

Magnetic mines dropped by the Germans were always a problem and one in Walton killed a direct descendant of John Hawkins, the Elizabethan Ships Captain, who was trying to defuse it. On Bramble Island behind Walton there was an Explosives factory,which was surrounded by mines. One blew up, and two locals killed when trying to rescue their dog.

For many years it was believed there was a spy living in Walton. Who this was, only they know, although the locally employed staff at the Von Ribbontrop home were all suspect. The job the spies did, wasn't that good, as they seemed unaware that numerous Submarines being towed past Walton were all made of wood to fool the enemy, and produced in Wivenhoe. Even Lord Haw-Haw the voice of the German Radio announced when one parted from it's tow rope, and became beached near Gt. Holland, that 'the submarine pens of Holland on Sea would receive a visit' and the area was machine gunned some days later, although nothing was made in Holland.

Everywhere was effected by this War. South Terrace in Walton, built in 1861 was completly destroyed in 1940, and was never rebuilt. The Pier was also attacked on one occasion.

On the Naze there was a secret Rocket Launcher under the Command of Colonel Burls. This experimental weapon was tried and tested from 1944 through to mid 1945. Each launch was completed with every piece of the rocket being gathered and inspected by the scientists.

As war in Germany ended and the cheering began, and on VE Night

137

(Victory in Europe) it was commemorated throughout the country.

That at Walton was held on the Naze, and a large blaze with effergies of Hitler, Goebbals and Mussolini on top. A Home Guard decided to make things even more impressive by throwing some smoke bombs into the flames, which, because of the extreme heat, turned the smoke red, and many were to go home with red faces and red clothes because of it.

A postscript to the war, was that over the following years, most of a Spitfire and various parts of other Aircraft have been found buried within the Naze.

On a more serious note, a year after the war, two council workers found two unexploded mines. One of these killed one of the men and the second badly injured the other.

Chapter 14 A THOUSAND YEARS OF WEATHER

The potential of good weather is a major selling factor regarding this coastline. Many hours of sunshine ensure people benifit from their stay and longevity is the watchword of many of the elderly.

In recent years the gap in the Ozone layer and the 'Greenhouse effect' are suggested reasons for the potential criteria for weather change, and yet nobody can ascertain whether the hole in the atmosphere hasn't always been there, for everything that is happening now, has happened before. In the 1970's and in the 1990's knowledgeable scientists were stating an Ice Age is due. In 1953, during the terrible year of flood and storm, there were similar scientists stating that we were then seeing the effect of the atomic bomb. On previous occasions and over the centuries the reasons for our weather have always been blamed on Volcanoes and Earthquakes in various parts of the world.

The pull of the moon, or storms on the sun, are now considered as creating many of the major problems here on earth, and again, all of these, are similar in effect and experience to those that have all happened on previous occasions. The phrase often recorded is that something is 'the worst in living memory', which is often correct, because with man living in an earlier age to no more than sixty or seventy, then as most disasters happen generally once or twice a century they would have only experienced

138

these events just once in their lives, and it would have been the worst in their memories. Over the centuries, weather records have improved, and now Television highlights a catastrophe frequency , which gives the impression that there appear to be far more taking place, when in fact there no more than there always have been.

The earliest known record of flooding within the area, was in November 1099 when the water rose to a height 'no man had seen before', yet flooding within Britain, hurricanes, earthquakes, drastic wind or exceedingly heavy rainstorms have been noted from the year 4 AD when a monk recorded that five hours of continual heavy downpour created massive damage in London.

There has been over the last thousand years at least once, every one hundred years, a record of Hurricanes or High Tides ravaging the countryside and many periods when too much rain has ruined crops or continual sunshine has created drought. The Thames has often dried up, and people have walked from oneside of London to the other, on the river bed. Generally most of the serious events have been recorded as they simply effected everyone.

Because of where we are, and during a time when few were actually interested in the welfare of those living here, only a handful of documents tell us about this area or give any specific reference, although we know that in 1237 flooding caused the death of many animals on the marshland at Holland. Therefore the more general weather reports effecting parts of both Britain and Western Europe would, it is surmised, have also effected this part of the country as well, and so the years 1362, 1570, 1588, 1695 are reported as Hurricane winds swept across Europe and throughout Britain and in it's wake created the deaths of thousands, and accordingly these storms would have produced major problems locally as well, based on the overal severity of these winds recorded elsewhere. The 1588 hurricane was advantageous to Britain because it devistated the Spanish Armada in the North Sea.

We know that storms with Hailstones over two inches (some reported to be over three inches) in diameter happened in 1260 and 1748 and these were reported in various parts of the country, and there are dozens of other examples recorded where they have ranged from the size and shape of peas, to measuring up to at least one and a half inches across. There have been

139

many times when periods of continual rain have continued non-stop (or so it seemed) for up to as much as 100 days. The summer of 1460 was recorded as being the wettest in over a century.

We know that heavy Thunderstorms on the 20th August 1691 created major problems within this area and a month later even worse storms were noted in mid-September of the same year, yet the rest of the country appears uneffected.

1662 provided massive hurricane winds. Daniel Defore wrote about the problems they caused and how they effected many parts of the Country, and on that occasion three Churches were actually destroyed (they were blown down), but he was to write far more in 1703, when the storms then were just as serious. It was his visual record that showed it was this storm, in November 1703, that in the Southern part of Britain there were over 8000 people who died. Over 2 million pounds worth of damage to Houses and property in London alone. Over 500 ships wrecked and the Eddystone Lighthouse was completly demolished. Over 17,000 Trees were uprooted in Kent. Flooding also enhanced the problems, and in Frinton, the Church was a victim of the storm, with the Bell Tower being being pushed over and much of the church was destroyed. Locally many buildings were blown down and farms were flattened.

There were very high Tides creating various degrees of flooding in 1738/9, 1756, 1786 and in 1791, when the flooding was aggrivated by a deep Snow fall, and Frost was to cover the country until the May. Many people died.

In 1812 a serious high tide flooded Holland Marshes. No animals were lost on that occasion but both animals and people died in 1813 when it was so cold that a Frost Fair was held on exceedingly thick Ice on the Thames in central London. Stalls were set up and entertainments went on for weeks. That year there was in total 14 weeks of non-stop Snow, Frost and Ice. Yet this event was not insular, for there had been similar times recorded, going back to 134 AD when the Ice on the Thames remained for over two months, and every forty or fifty years this excessive cold spell was to be repeated throughout the period 100 AD to 1813. Adverse weather and freak events continually have happened. In 1413 it even snowed as late as April 9th, which was King Henry V's Coronation day.

140

In 1815 more flooding, then in late 1836 a Hurricane during the winter period produced eight foot high snowdrifts in Walton and Kirby, and a frost was to cover the countryside for three months. In that year there were Five shipwrecks at Walton because of these storms. Mails took two and three days to get through during the worst period, and this continued into 1837 with a frost that remained for over two months and the death of many people throughout the Country.

On 5th April 1839 High Tides do massive damage and in 1840 downpours of rain create more flooding. Over 90 acres within Great and Little Holland were under water, covering farm land and marshes. That year there was continual rain without interuption. Tops of gateposts were seen just above the level of the water in some places.

In Dec 1846 there was again serious flooding, and yet a year earlier, January had been so mild that wheat had started to grow and roses blossomed. It was one of the driest years for nearly a century, and then severe Frosts were to start in November and continued until late February, which was to be exacerbated by flooding.

Tidal damage in 1853. In 1855 a dreadful 'Tempest and Hailstorm' broke windows and many buildings were damaged. In Oct. 1863 winds take the top off Holland Windmill, and the Tide rose to four or five feet higher than normal in March 1874, killing hundreds of sheep on the marshes. In 1878 it rained everyday for months and it was a cold spring as well, ensuring crops were ruined. In that same year the tide on one occasion went so low it went out nearly a 1000 metres (over 3000 feet) from the shoreline, and it was at West Point, then five miles from the town of Walton, that rubble from buildings were discovered on the Sea Bed, which indicates how serious the erosion of the land has been at the Naze.

Storms in 1881 brought about the collapse of the original Pier and the South Window of Frinton Church blew in, but not one piece of glass was damaged. There was more flooding in Nov. 1882 and serious storms had stopped the Regatta that year, and in 1897 the Seas breached Sea Walls in over thirty places when a Tornado hit Frinton and Waltons coastline. In 1906 there was more continuous rain, and in July 1927, because at that time Frinton Tennis Courts had no drainage, water was up to the tops of the nets and the Tournement that year had to be cancelled. March in 1931 was the coldest in over sixty years. 1948, 1953 and 1967 all had varied aspects of flooding, but there have been many occasions when serious winds have taken away Beach Huts, tiles and fences, and the hurricane winds of 1987 uprooting most of the country.

Gunfleet Sands two thousand years ago was part of the shore line, and may possibly have even been inland, but by 1628 a Bouy was needed to try and ensure wrecks would be curtalied on what had become dangerous sand banks. During the war with the Dutch in the 17th Century, Boats on both sides, record being aware of the Bouy. It was even suggested to the Military that it should be removed, so the Dutch would flounder on these Sands, but it was then ascertained that the British Boats might also have the same problem.

In 1884 there was a major earthquake that created havoc throughout the country, yet major tremours were also felt in 1692 and 1755 and in June 1931 people in Walton stated they remembered being thrown from one side of a room to the other. This area did escape massive damage, yet earthquakes have been recorded as early as 1114. The severity of the April 24th 1884 Earthquake can be assessed with 1200 homes and 31 Churches/Chapels being seriously damaged within Colchester.

The Health of people locally has been generally good. Whilst full details of the Black Death in 1348, are not known, over a quarter of the population in Colchester died of the Plague in 1665, with between 4700 and 5000 dying this way, yet whilst the country was twice ravaged by epidemics of Cholera, and in 1849, within London, over 15,000 died, in Kirby, Walton, Frinton and Gt. Holland there were no cases at all, nor were there any cases five years later in 1854 when it struck again. Foot and Mouth effected animals throughout Britain in 1865. None of the cattle in this area were effected.

In 1837 the weather was so bad, that, at the Hall in Gt. Holland, out of a staff of twenty, ten men and two boys were all down with Influenza at the same time. This 'flu' bug was to kill people throughout the country, and whilst many were effected, none were to die in this area as far is as known. In late 1918 when the 'Flu Bug' swept across Europe and was to kill millions, with very many thousands in Britain, again no deaths from this cause are listed locally.

142

Nothing in weather change is new. It has all happened before. Months of bitter freezing cold. Weeks of continual rain. Snow eight feet deep. Heat that ensures nothing grows. Water shortage. Flooding, and always there are those seeking an answer as to the reason for these repeated disasters. A general appreciation of weather history indicates that nothing in the future will change, for what will be, will be.

One myth that needs to be crushed, is that during the last fifty years there has only been five White Christmas's throughout the South East of England, and statements suggesting there have been many, are known to be built on dodgy memories and wishful thinking. Looking back two hundred years shows there has only been an average of one in every ten years when snow has fallen at the right time, showing that imagination does not always go hand in hand with the truth.

Nothing has changed. It's not the Atomic Bomb, nor men on the moon, but an understanding that shows the weather is a law unto itself even until doomsday, which according to prophecy, could be in eight or eight hundred years, when comets from outer space come rushing towards us, creating panic, and then, their course changes and everyone gives a big sigh of relief and the Churches start to empty again.

FRINTON, KIRBY, GT. HOLLAND and WALTON will continue to exist and man may attempt to make changes but if they do not, then the Naze will definitely fall to the Sea and a large bay will be created where the backwaters now exist. At that time, the villages of Beaumont, Gt. Oakley and Kirby Le Soken will be under threat and Walton will be under attack from the North West, with every major storm or flooding assisting the massive erosion that is happening continually, but life will go on.

Maybe man will be eventually be living on the Moon when the Naze disappears, but he will still not be able to alter the Weather, and he will still be saying to his children that 'I remember when I was a boy, we always had hot summers and it always snowed at Christmas'.

Chapter 15 ADDENDUM -
The biggest mystery of them all!

As the last pages of this book were being put together, and the final dots put into place, additional information continued to arrive.

Many of the items have been added to these pages, but there were others that were 'non essentials' and none warrented a complete re-write of any of the chapters. Then one small monograph came to hand, that needed reconfirmation and at the same time to give a greater understanding of the statements made in the first two Chapters. Therefore, this book ends with the period it started with, regarding the formative years of the area, particularly the 'SOKENS'

Based on a calligraphers examination of the early Manuscripts held by St. Pauls, the most important Document to us, which shows Eadulvanaesa had been given to St. Pauls by King Athelston, when compared to others covering a period of at least 150 years, up to the 1050's, was found to have been written in the hand of a single scribe, suggesting that the true original(s) were destroyed when the Church of St. Pauls was gutted by fire (c1087 AD)

Accordingly, this important existing Manuscript appears to have been written during the period 1090/1120, and is possibly an amalgamation of Manuscripts that had also been destroyed in the fire, combining Walton, Kirby and Thorpe with a number of other estates, and all, purporting to have originated from King Athelston. Originally these parcels of land were probably given to St. Pauls by various people, and accordingly the Thorpe, Kirby and Walton package may have had nothing to do with King Athelston.

Even the name EADULVANAESA is also possibly incorrect other than this could have been the name locals were calling their area. It is probable that few of the Monks or scribes would have had any reason to have examined the original Manuscripts prior to the fire and if they had, they would have been quite unable to repeat from memory what they had contained, and therefore impossible to re-write verbateum.

Had King William hinted he was due to set in motion a survey of all the lands the Churches owned (?), and, after the fire, did the Monks of St. Pauls panic when they realized they did not have any documentation covering a number of areas, and which the crown might take without proof.

144

It is possible that the Estate did have a name similar to Edulvasnasesa, because it is mentioned as such within other earlier documents, but it could have been based on the Latin spelling of Audulvasnasa, as given in the Domesday Book. How and where this originated is unknown. It is possible that the Romans gave it a similar name five hundred years earlier. It could as easilly have been given by the Saxons or even by the Danes when they overran this section of the country.

Until such time as the area was split and sold, the land of Thorpe, Walton and Kirby was basically one Estate which had three Churches, and which had, at some time been split into 'Manors'. We consider Eadulvanaesa as a single area of land, although it was three manors, because it was depicted as such during most visitations by St. Pauls. They only became independent areas from the 1500's onwards when the lands were sold as seperate Estates.

The date suggested when this land was given to St. Pauls has now to be queried, and no longer can the year be simply 'pre-940', for this is a date that is based on what is known about King Athelston, yet, the lands could have been passed to St. Pauls a hundred or even five hundred years earlier (c440 to 840 AD), but certainly not later than the 950's as the monks would not have quoted King Athelston as their benifactor. It is shown in one Medieval Document, that St. Pauls had 'always had the lands of Eadulvanaesa', suggesting they were passed to St. Pauls at a very early date.

What is needed is someone with good working knowledge of Latin and Saxon, and some early Danish and, more important, having a lot of time on their hands, to start re-reading exactly what is stated within all the existing Manuscripts, starting with those held by the Guildhall Library on behalf of St. Pauls.

The possibilities of establishing new detail may seem remote, and yet, unless someone knows what they are looking for, then a previously incorrect translation by an early Archivist can be established, and if read with understanding, it may provide far greater alacrity of when, and even why, St. Pauls were really given these lands, and at that time, a major 'local' mystery that has remained paramount for over a 1000 years, might eventually be solved.

Chapter 16   LAND OWNERSHIP TO 1765
(according to Morant) and
POPULATION 1801 to 1901
(according to the Census)

The following list is basically MORANT lists of 1765 giving the names of the owners of the various Estates within the area. New names can be added to these which he did not have, and accordingly a few have been included although there are more, as show within Chapters 1 and 2. It was not the intention of this book to list hundreds of names, as very few mean anything, other than to a Geneologist looking for a relative

Period of ownership   Family Name
                                                         Owning Estate/Lands
FRINTON:

Originally it was in two Manors, one owned by King Harold.

In Edward the Confessors time :   Levefin
Domesday Book   :   Geoffrey de Magnaville
                                                    and Eustace Earl of Bologne
During reign of King Henry ll   :   Tregoz of Tollefhunt (Lord D'Arcy)

About this time, it reverted to the single Manor:

In King Edwards lst reign   :   De Burnham who had been
                                                    married to Alice Tregoz
In 1392   :   John Rokele
In 1421   :   Geoffrey de Rockett or Rokele
In 1426   :   John Godmanston passed
                                                    to William Godmanston
                                                    (who fell in battle)
In 1473   :   Joanne the Widow of William
                                                    remarried to Gilbert Hussy

146

In 1498	:	Phillipa, sister of William, who received the land when Joanne died
In early 1500's	:	Sir Ralph Chamberlain then passed to
In 1576	:	Granddaughter Mary Gray
In 1585	:	Passed to her daughter Dorothy, who married William Perton of Little Bentley
In c 1600	:	Edward Grimton also owned the Manor Frinton Hall. Everything to his son then to the Grandson, Sir Harbottle Grimton
In 1691	:	Thomas Warren, a Mariner passed to his son in law James Bushnall, who willed it to his son Jeremy Bushnall
c1700	:	Sir Richard Hopkins
c1720	:	Sir Edward Bellamy
c.1740's	:	George Lynne of Southwick

KIRBY

There have only been four manors within Kirby, with two of these coming within the lands that were part of the Eadulvesnaesa Estate.

The Manor of Kirby and the The Manor of Grove House were part of the St. Pauls Estate (with Walton and Thorpe) given to the Church it is believed before 930/940 AD (see Chapter 15).

The Manors of Snedding Hall and Birch Hall were both seperate Estates. Birch Hall was for centuries linked with Horsey Island, although during these early centuries Horsey was not an Island (or a group of Islands) but a large expanse of land held together with streams and rivers crossing it. (See Frontis map) Both were also, at one point to be owned seperately by

St. Pauls and each having a Special Jurisdiction. Neither were part of the Eadulvesnaesa Estate/ Lands.

THE MANOR OF KIRBY

Until 1551	:	St. Pauls London then passed
		by the King Edward Vl to Thos. DArcy
		and his heirs - This included :
		John Lord Darcy; The Savage Family;
		Lord Rochford
c1775	:	Robert Rigby

Part of the lands were sold to John La Motte who then gave them to his daughter, Lady Hester, who was married to Sir Thomas Honywood. They passed to Lt. Gen. Phillip Honywood who owned other lands within the area at this time.

MANOR OF GROVE HOUSE

Until 1551	:	St. Pauls, London
In 1559	:	Sir John Reynesforth lived here
In 1630	:	Robert Alefounder of Dedham
		then passed to his son Robert

The Two above Estates continued to be linked together when John Shaw purchased both between 1630 and 1700.
Members of the Shaw family retained the House and Estate, then it passed to.

c1770	:	Elizabeth who married John King
		Their son Shaw King
		retained the property
c1775	:	Robert Rigby

148

MANOR OF SNEDDON HALL

Pre-1000   :   St. Pauls London

The list of owners was unknown by Morant
                    The Sneating Family took over the Hall at one time.

THE MANOR OF BIRCH HALL

Prior to the Norman Conquest, Ingelric rented this Manor from St. Pauls

Pre-1OOO   :   St. Pauls
In 1050   :   Eustace Earl of Bolougne
                                              Had been taken from St. Pauls
                                              as a grant to the Earl.

Between 11OO and 1437   :   Was passed to St. Osyths
                                                          Monastry
In 1539   :   Henry Vlll passed it to
                                              Thomas Lord Cromwell
                                              but it remained
                                                      Crown property.
1564 (June 24th)   :   Elizabeth 1st passed
                                              it to Henry Fanshawe
Between then and 17OO   :   The Fanshawes retained
                                              the building but it changed
                                              ownership name when
                                              Mary Fanshawe
                                              Married Sir Thomas Campbell
Early in 17OO's   :   John Batch

HORSEY belongs to the BIRCH HALL Estate.

In 1750 John Bloss had the Estate.

GT HOLLAND (originally 'Holland' before being split)

Originally owned by King Alfred and King Edward the Elder
(see Chapter 2)

Edward Confessors time	:	LeFstan
1050	:	Walter de Doai
Beginning of Edward 1st	:	Robert Burnel
		(Bishop of Bath and Wells and Lord Chancellor)
1294	:	Philip Burnel passed Estate to Edward Lord Burnel
	:	Various Burnels followed through female side or the Male

In 1461 (4th March) King Edward IV gave the Lands to
        Henry Bouchier, Earl of Essex
In 1551 King Edward VI passed the Manor and church to
        Sir Thomas Darcy

	:	Various Darcy's until 1639
Up to c1700	:	Joseph Thurston
	:	Sold to Daniel Bayley
	:	who sold to Sir Richard Hopkins and his widow sold it
In 1748	:	To Robert Martin
In 1763	:	Daughter married to John Kirby

Others owning lands in the parish in 1760 included Samuel Holditch;
Samuel Newton and John Blowers

WALTON

The Manor of Walton (including the Naze:)
Possibly between 930/940   : Dean and Chapter of St. Pauls.

150

In 1551	:	Passed to Thomas Lord Darcy
c1650	:	Earl Rivers Believed to have lost the ownership at cards to
		Rt Hon Earl of Rochford
c1775	:	Robert Rigby

The other Estates within Walton include:

In 1765 Walton Ashes was owned by Philip Bennet who owned also another farm
Considerable estates in Walton and Kirby were owned by Shaw King (see above) There was in 1765 an Estate owned by John Wheely or Wheeler
John Bernard and William Stone have also lands in the Parish.

POPULATION

1801 to 1901

Name of the Town:	Acreage:	Year:	No. of people:
FRINTON	469 Acres	1801	31
Little growth until:		1871	54
		1881	57
		1891	87
		1901	644
		1911	1510
		1921	3032
GREAT HOLLAND	2104 Acres	1801	300
		1851	508
		1901	413

151

KIRBY   3859 Acres 1801   664
  (including Le Soken, Cross, and Horsey Islands)
Between 1811 and 1901 an average number of 900

WALTON   2146 Acres 1801   221
  Rapid growth begins in   1851   729
                                1871   1070
                                1901   2014

The above is a brief summary of the growth figures within all four areas,
but where there was little growth, then just the one figure has been stated
(Kirby) and Gt. Holland shows how little growth took place. Walton was
around the 200 to 300 figure for forty years then there was a rapid growth
as shown, Frintons started from 1881 onwards, and this is why the
years 1911 and 1921 are included.

   Population figures were often given within Guide Books but on occasions
these were not always correct, and some appear to be pure guesswork.
They are also to be found in the Kellys Directories whose population figures
are normally reasonably close, and of course, there were the ten yearly
Census figures.

BIBLIOGRAPHY

It is a normal practice at this point to name all the sources that have been used within the production of this book, not only the people who have assisted, but also the names of the books and articles used. Yet, where this is concerned, based on over 1000 works that have been examined, plus the long list of individual voices that have freely given information, it would add at least ten and possibly twenty pages for every source to be listed, and to each I give my apologises for not including their name.

Yet a general overall thanks has to be given to the compilors of the Domesday Book and then over the centuries everyone from then on with a special thanks to Dr. Peter Boyden. Therewere a few references before Domesday, but these and many others are included in Peter Boydens marvelous collection of monographs, as he has, between 1963 and the present time, gathered more information about Walton and this area than anyone, and more important, he has included verbatum the words and comments of past writers.

Therefore. Utalising everything that could be attained and read. Double checking and confirming the comments, remarks and statements of hundreds of people, this book has aimed to provide and produce new detail, as well as trying to correct the many statements that have appeared in the past and which in some cases are still being repeated within even the most recent publications at this time.

I suggest that any student wishing to go deeper into this subject read Peter Boydens monographs and follow up the references he lists. These are all fine stepping stones into local history, yet once checked, new ones are to be found and so you will move onwards, as there are still many more. I have to repeat my sincere thanks again to the very many people who have all assisted with the loan of items or information gathered, and to them I give my thanks here in writing.

In addition there are the Libraries. Frinton, Walton, Clacton, Colchester, Guildhall. The British Library, British Museum and Public Records Office. Both Essex Records Offices. The RNLI, Salvation Army, Trinity House and many others. They have all added to the story enfolded within these pages.

Yet it must be stressed. As time has progressed new information regarding such old subject matter, has been formulated by reading and utalising the innumerable diaries, monographs, books, letters and sources that have arisen from the backs of cupboards or in attics and which in some cases have not seen the light of day since they were stored many years earlier and which provide previously unknown information or detail.

Accordingly, when new material does come to hand, and there appear to be conflicts in previous statements, then this has needed further investigation where ever possible. The few books that have been written about this area have all suffered from the same problem, whereby, in a lot of instances they have not looked deep enough, nor have they understood the changes in land mass that have taken place over the last few thousand years.

A long selling book on Britain still continues to state that the old Cburch of Walton fell to the waves in 1798. This has been repeated in too many books which mention Walton. As has been shown, this is yet another figment of to many writers imaginations because they have not bothered to do any research. Once stated, always repeated.

Because of it's status, the Victoria History of Essex is taken to be correct, and it is as such, classified as an important work showing all four communities. Writers therefore do not query any of it's statements either, and repeat exactly what it shows, and yet, as pages 35/36 in Volume 2 dealing with Walton, the Victoria simply took it for granted that if the writing produced from Copperas on manuscripts was black, then the Ink that had been used, must also have been black. Again insufficient thought had been utalised to query that if the Ink in liquid form was a bright Transparent Blue, how did it manage to produce Black writing.

A great amount of research has been done by the author and yet he is aware that tomorrow, or next week or next year, new information will come to hand which will change and alter the outcome of a small number of things that are included here. Such is the problem with 'Local History'

A perfect example of this, is that the author admits that his previous book, and also as shown in two Videos, there were small errors, and which were established as such after publication. All of these were corrected with each book or Video, as they came out.

154

It is hoped this book will be seen as the 'definitive' book regarding this area for a few years to come, although, it is known that by the time this is published a few new alternate areas of information might be forthcoming, and a word or a phrase will in later editions will need to be corrected.

If you see anything that you believe is wrong or incorrect, please get in touch, although everything indicated has, in most cases, been triple checked and yet there will be someone reading this who will believe they know differently to that which has been stated.

If you have anything at all, be it articles, monographs, books, diaries, newspapers, photographs, etchings, drawings or Postcards, even original negatives, glass or film, please indicate to Ken Palmer so he can make copies and return them to you. Old Movie films: 9.5mm, 8mm, 16mm and other sizes, as well as Video material, are all required urgently. Home movies are wanted always, so copies can be made, and he will normally provide a free Video copy if everything is straight forward when returning the original material back to you.

Telephone Ken Palmer on O1255 674224. The negatives of everything that are copied will eventually be handed to the Essex Records Office, to enable future generations to see what exists, and therefore anything and everything you have, needs to be seen and examined.

If you have something to add, be it old memories or a few pictures, then get in touch. If on the other hand, you can offer nothing, then it makes no matter. Simply enjoy this book, and discover a world gone by.

INDEX

Also Available:

A BOOK: 'WISH YOU WERE HERE IN'
                    FRINTON, KIRBY and WALTON

A COFFEE TABLE STYLE BOOK OF PHOTOGRAPHS . IT ALSO INCLUDES A LOT OF WRITTEN MATERIAL NOT INCLUDED WITHIN THIS PRESENT VOLUME

TWO VIDEOS;
FRINTON, KIRBY and WALTON   Vol. 1
FRINTON, GT. HOLLAND, KIRBY and WALTON   Vol. 2

TWO VIDEOS SHOWING MANY DIFFERENT PHOTOGRAPHS NOT INCLUDED WITHIN EITHER OF THE BOOKS. THEY ALSO INCLUDE ORIGINAL FOOTAGE FROM EARLY HOME MOVIES COVERING A PERIOD 1928 TO 1980's